TRANSFORM YOUR LIFE
WITH THE
VIOLET FLAME

A Practical Guide

THE VIOLET FLAME

TRANSFORM
YOUR LIFE
WITH THE
VIOLET FLAME

A Practical Guide

Hilary Stanley

Talking

Whoever holds the talking
stick has within their
hands the sacred
power of words –
only the one
who holds the
stick may
speak

but
must
speak the
truth about
personal
understanding
and experience

Stick

First published in Great Britain by
Talking Stick
an imprint of Archive Publishing
Dorset England

For all our titles please go to:
transpersonalbooks.com

A CIP Record for this book is available from
the British Cataloguing in Publication data office

ISBN 978-1-906289-25-6   (Paperback)

To contact the author, please visit her website
www.hilarystanley.co.uk

Printed and bound
around the globe
by LSI

THE AUTHOR

Hilary had a spiritual family background and followed an artistic and creative career. Work, marriage and children took precedence over her spiritual life until she became friendly with a Medium who taught Hilary to meditate, and encouraged her along her spiritual path.

At some point Hilary remembered seeing and hearing Spirit as a child, and frequently had experiences of travelling out-of-body. Gradually those memories and good guidance from teachers here in the physical world, helped her to learn and understand more of Life throughout Time and other dimensions. She also studied and journeyed with many Spirit Guides and Beings of other realms.

Her passion for the Violet Flame has helped her to cope and adapt to life's challenges, and she enjoys teaching and encouraging others on their own spiritual journeys. The Violet Flame was the inspiration behind 'Amethyst', a shop, healing and teaching centre in Bournemouth which she set up and ran for three years.

Now Hilary is a grandmother, without the responsibility of 'Amethyst', she works from her home in Dorset. She is a Reiki Master/Teacher, Crystal Healer, Shamballa Multidimensional Healer and Psychic Surgeon. She reads the Thoth Tarot Cards, offers Past Lives Readings and channels Spirit Guides to help and advise others.

In recent years her fascination has grown with the science of energy and the workings of the Universe. She sees the meeting of Spirituality and Science like the unison of the Heart and Mind, and feels they are drawing ever closer!

To contact the author, please visit her website
www.thevioletflame.co.uk
or: www.hilarystanley.co.uk

DEDICATION

With enormous gratitude to
Emma Cutler
for getting me started, typing, creating order and structure,
and supplying the chocolate!

Also:
Jennifer Sheldon
for proof reading and editing
and
Walter Bruneel
for the cover image.

*I dedicate this book to all those who have helped, guided,
and shared this journey with me, and particularly to all my
friends, my family, children and grandchildren.*

Note from the author:

*"To achieve balance and harmony, the Violet Flame is the best
tool we have. It will transform us and our world from this present state
to a more enlightened, spiritual way of being where we can transmute
all doubts, fears or negative energy to positive creativity. If we so
choose.*

*Transmute every negative thought and emotion to resonate with the
vibration of the Violet Flame – for that is the frequency of energy that
will transform your life!*

*As with all things, discernment is important. maybe not all of this book
will resonate with each of you. I urge you to accept what feels right
in your heart and leave the rest for another time or another
person".*

Hilary Stanley

CONTENTS

Foreword   13

PART ONE:
Basic information and practical applications   15

Chapter 1   17
What is the Violet Flame?
Why is it the colour of Violet?
A violet aura
Why is it a Flame?
How does it work?
The power of Thought, Intent and Will
Summary

Chapter 2   27
Where does the Violet Flame come from?
How the Violet Flame evolved
What does it do? –
     Freedom from Dis-ease
     Mercy, Justice and Forgiveness for emotional balance
     Justice to settle karmic debts
     Transmutation of negative thoughts for mental ease
     Transmutation of negative environmental energy
     Sacred Ceremony to enhance spiritual connection
     It's just Magic!
Summary

Chapter 3   39
Preparing to work with the Violet Flame
     Get ready – preparation
     Get Set – grounding
     Go – ignite the spark
Summary

Chapter 4   47
Ways to work with the Violet Flame
      Visualisation and meditation
      Decrees, mantras and affirmations
      Writing   – To release
                – To manifest
                – To see the truth and potential
      Being creative, drawing and painting
      Creating a sacred space
      Using crystals
      Aura sprays and incense
Summary

Chapter 5   65
Incorporating the Violet Flame into your daily life
      Keeping the 'spark' alight
      Clearing and protecting spaces
      Infusing food, drink and water
      Crystals
      Music, song and dance
Summary

PART TWO:
Using the Violet Flame in specific areas of life   73

Chapter 6   75
Relationships:
      Attract the right relationship
      Laying the foundations
      Harmony and equality
      Dealing with difficulties
                – Conflicts and arguments
                – Gossip and misunderstandings
                – Outside influences – family and friends

Endings – Natural
– Created
– Dealing with – Fear and guilt
– Anger and bewilderment
– Loss and emptiness
Closure/Moving on
Summary

Chapter 7   95
Job/Career Matters
Self employment
Finding the right line of work
Promotion and marketing
Preparing for success
Facing difficulties
Expectations
Adjusting to change
Dealing with major disputes
Seeking employment
Applying for jobs
Attending interviews
In employment
Harmony
Stress – Anger and Frustration
– Rules and Regulations
– Unequal workload
– Unrealistic demands
– Moving up, down, sideways and out
Promotion
Restructures
Redundancy
Retirement
Summary

Chapter 8   125
Health and Wellbeing

Cause and Effect
Physical Injury or Illness
Mental Wellbeing
    Confidence/self esteem
    Changing patterns of behaviour
    Changing habits
Emotional Balance
    Connecting heart and mind
    Fears and Phobias
    Mending a broken heart
    Bereavement – Passing peacefully
                  – Suddenly gone
                  – Dealing with grief
Summary

Chapter 9   149
Healing
    Healing Exercise for Self and Others – Chakra clearing
    Violet Flame combined with Reiki
    Healing with Violet Flame crystals
    Sending/Distance Healing
    Planetary Healing
    Healing for Animals, Nature, and the Elementals
Summary

Chapter 10   169
Past Lives and Karma
    Skills, talents, traits and families
    Clearing the debts   – To others
                       – To our own soul
    Karma from previous lifetimes
    Old wounds and scars
    The Akashic Records
    Karma from this lifetime
    Earth's karma
Summary

Chapter 11   199
Past, Present and Future
    From the beginning
    Now
    Lighten up!
    And so it goes on...

Glossary   203

Acknowledgements   211

FOREWORD

*I imagined myself surrounded by Violet Light.
I breathed in deeply and imagined the Violet Light spreading
through me.
I breathed out what I imagined was dirty grey air, taking all
my worries and concerns with it. Soon I was breathing in
Violet Light and breathing out Violet Light.
The outer edge of the Violet Light around me formed into a
bubble and I felt myself floating upwards, the Earth drifting by
beneath me. I was totally at peace, carried along in my violet
bubble, no cares or anxiety intruded here. Any everyday
thoughts were immediately transmuted within the Violet Ray
to a calm acceptance of a higher purpose, so any worrying
was futile.
I felt my bubble of Violet Light begin to float gently back
down to Earth and as it settled, I was aware of the beautiful,
oriental Goddess of mercy and compassion, Kuan Yin,
standing before me. She held an empty silver dish in her
delicate, outstretched hands. She asked me to take it, look
deeply into it and tell her what I could see. At first, the
answer was simple – it was an empty dish!
Just as I was about to say "Nothing", I hesitated.*

*A change in the light seemed to cause a flicker, a very slight
glow in the dish. I waited to see if it would grow or change,
before I gave her an answer. I don't know how long we stood
there, she waiting patiently, me gazing into a seemingly
empty dish, but the longer I stared into it, the more certain I
became that I could see a light flickering like a tiny tea light
candle flame. It was faintly violet coloured. The more I
accepted what I could see, the stronger the flame grew until
it was really there, a Violet Flame alight and burning in my
"empty" dish. I didn't want to look away from it in case it
disappeared, so told Kuan Yin what I could see, without*

looking up.
She said, "You know it is there, it will always be there
whenever you look, so it is alright to look away now.
Whenever you need it, you know where to find it."
With that, she blew the Violet Flame directly into my heart
chakra, and there it has stayed.
It glows within me, sometimes faintly, sometimes very
strongly as if I AM the Violet Flame, but I know it is there and
it is always there whenever I look, whenever I need it.

This was my introduction to the Violet Flame. It has changed my life

Following this experience I read a little about the Violet Flame, learning that repeating decrees or mantras many times would build the energy to work on whatever was appropriate. However, that didn't feel quite right for me personally so I meditated asking my own Spirit Guides for further information. Since then the Flame itself has flickered, grown and evolved into what we know now. Over the years I have run many workshops and written articles on this subject and eventually I felt the need to write a book. So here it is... I hope you enjoy it, use it, and let it become part of your life, as it has become such a great part of mine.

PART ONE

The following is an excerpt from *The Masters and Their Retreats* by Mark L. Prophet and Elizabeth Clare Prophet. It was information channelled by them from Arcturus and Victoria, the Elohim of the Seventh, or Violet Ray of Light. They urge us to use the Violet Flame in any way that inspires us.

> *"The Violet Flame is the wonder drug of the century and it can make a difference as to which way planet Earth goes.*
>
> *I don't mind if you whistle the Violet Flame, sing the Violet Flame, jump and dance to the Violet Flame, do circle dances to all of your music to the Violet Flame, create new music to the Violet Flame decrees. I don't mind whatever you do. Make games out of it! Do marathons with it! But whatever you do, beloved ones, you have to get busy with exciting and innovative methods to bring that Violet Flame into every area of your life.*
>
> *So you will decide whether the Violet Flame shall be for you, the point of the springboard of your victory, turning around your life and your outlook. Everything that happens to you in this world can be altered by the Violet Flame. Only you can decide! "*

...So let's get going!...

Part One covers the basic information, practical applications and suggestions for building the Violet Flame energy within you. I would recommend that you read all of this section and familiarise yourself with the energy, incorporating it into your life in any way that feels right for you and then apply it to any specific aspects or issues, as discussed in Part Two.

Please do not feel you have to try all the methods – remember they are only suggestions. I do hope you will be inspired to find new ways to transform your life, your world and our planet.

There is no right or wrong way to use the Violet Flame, as it will only work for the Highest Good. When you incorporate an element of fun and enjoyment and use it regularly, it works even better. It is not solely for spiritual advancement; that happens naturally as you start to transform your daily life. Changes will happen bit by bit until you find that your life has become your soul's purpose, you are fulfilling your destiny and feel complete.

All you need is a desire to change and the will to make it happen; the Violet Flame will do the rest.

A glossary has been created at the end for any terms which you may find unfamiliar.

CHAPTER 1

WHAT IS THE VIOLET FLAME?

The Violet Flame is energy of transformation

The energy of all living things vibrates or resonates at different rates. The frequency or speed of these vibrations relate to how we see colour, how we hear sound and how we feel or sense what is going on around us. These vibrations are the energy or the 'atmosphere' we pick up and react to subconsciously; they determine how we respond to other people and our environment.

The highest or fastest frequency vibration that we can normally detect corresponds to the colour violet. Violet is the highest frequency of light that we can see with the naked eye, the 'boundary' of our rainbow, beyond which light has other properties that we cannot see, like infrared and ultraviolet. So the energy of Violet Light is on the brink of change – from one state to another. When the Violet Light becomes sufficiently concentrated, the energy takes on form and shape, expanding and contracting as flames do. This highly concentrated Violet Light becomes the Violet Flame. It has life and energy of its own, with the power to burn away negativity, illuminate the darkness, energise and activate all other energy to create change.

We cannot change the whole world in an instant, but we can start by changing ourselves, just slight adjustments to our thoughts, our outlook and our interactions with others. As the frequency of our own vibration quickens and starts to resonate at the same level as Violet Light, a spark lights within us which grows into a flame and the glow of that flame spreads through us, around us and reaches out to others we come into contact with. If enough people here on Earth resonate at that frequency... then the world will start to change; peace, harmony and love will preside.

The energy of the Violet Flame is freely available to anyone. There are no 'attunements' or 'initiations'... it simply IS. The more you learn of it and the more you use it, the more you can achieve with it and the easier it becomes to transform your own life, those around you and your world.

For me personally, the Violet Flame has become my way of dealing with any issue in my life that I wish to change. Whether that is a matter of health, love, understanding, dealing with bureaucracy, helping other people, or anything else, I find the energy of the Violet Flame shifts perceptions, difficulties seem to find a solution and everything comes into balance. (There are many examples and personal experiences later in the book.)

You can take it anywhere!

Since I first felt the energy of the Violet Flame, I have incorporated it into my daily life as part of my morning routine. This was the easiest change to make! It feels natural, totally right for me and I now feel as if I live in the Violet Flame, it is within me, surrounds me, and I see others respond to the energy of it without knowing why!

One morning I was in the doctor's waiting room, surrounded by posters warning of various forms of cancer, flu, even malaria; it was a place full of fear. I looked around at the people waiting there almost mentally bombarded with the fear the posters were relaying. So I consciously focused on the Violet Flame within me, building it up, feeling its glow spreading throughout my physical body, pushing it out into my aura and expanding Violet Light out into the room. There were no visible changes to my physical body, (I wasn't breathing deeply with my eyes closed or sitting in a lotus position!) I just sat and watched the Violet Light spreading throughout the waiting room. Five separate people suddenly looked up and directly at me, so I smiled and they smiled back.

Did they know? I have no idea.
Did it matter? Not a bit!

I noticed the level of chatter rose; people seemed to relax as they talked to the person sitting next to them:
"Hasn't the weather been changeable lately?" I heard.
The irony of the fact that she used the word 'change' made me smile even more, and thankfully the nurse called me in, commenting it was quite lively in the waiting room this morning.

Why is this energy the colour of violet?

Violet is the highest or fastest frequency vibration of light; it is produced by a combination of blue and pink.

Separately, blue is the accepted spiritual colour of power, strength and protection. It represents divine will, the energy of intent. It is the driving force, the impetus.

Pink represents unconditional love, compassion, understanding and forgiveness.

Combining power and strength with love and compassion creates the energy to change and transform negativity for the best possible outcome. The colour of that combination is Violet.

Violet is on the boundary to the next 'octave' of light frequencies, we cannot see colour beyond the Violet Light of our rainbow. So it is the highest vibration of light that we can see with the naked eye. Beyond this are the realms of imagination, leading to unseen possibilities where we are inspired to create change.

Violet is also the colour of our crown (7th) chakra which overlaps the physical and spiritual dimensions and so acts as a doorway or channel to raise the vibration of our energy. Within this vibration we can access our Higher Selves, our Guides, other Ascended Masters and Teachers, Angels, Archangels and all Beings of Spiritual Light.

The energy will transfer us to and from this physical life. It has often been reported to me that a violet glow seems to fill the room when a loved one is departing this life, and I find these phenomena fascinating. They often come from people with no knowledge of the Violet Flame or even any particular spiritual beliefs, but rather they know me and know the colour violet is meaningful to me. I have always tried to explain the significance of this colour as a means of transformation, changing from this physical life to whatever comes next, according to their individual beliefs.

I am sure that the same happens when a baby is born into this life, although most parents and midwives probably never notice, with other things uppermost in their minds!

A violet aura

Many years ago when I was studying Reiki, I had an 'aura photo' taken. I was pleased to see that it was the bright emerald green of healing and particularly of Reiki energy. Over many years at Fayres and Festivals I have occasionally had another of these aura photos taken and seen it change from green to blue and quite dramatically to violet as I started to incorporate the Violet Flame into my life. These 'aura photos' capture a moment at rest, in the most natural state of your being and although your aura does change in reaction to different circumstances, the 'aura photo' does show your present and underlying energy field.

Some people are fortunate enough to be able to see others' auras or energy fields with their open eyes, in physical reality. I have been told by such people that they see Violet Light around me, even if they do not know of the Violet Flame and my association with it.

I once saw an artwork image entitled The Violet Flame Temple by Walter Bruneel and it took my breath away. It was just as I had seen it in my meditations, and of course I had to buy it! When I had the opportunity to meet Walter at an art and book-signing event, he apparently asked to meet the lady with the shiny violet aura! Needless to say, we became good friends and have worked together in many ways since.

Walter works a great deal with the Extended Violet Flame and creates all sorts of magical artwork of pure energy, light and colour. He created the cover image used for this book. (See the Acknowledgements at the back of the book for his website)

Why is it a Flame?

The energy is shown as a flame because fire is a known and accepted symbol of cleansing and transformation.

A flame is energy that is never still, it dances and grows, illuminating the darkness. It can not be contained. It needs air and space; freedom to burn. The Violet Flame is not static or fixed, but is constantly changing and evolving too.

Heat and fire can actually change or alter the form of anything; turning solid to liquid and liquid to steam. Similarly, the Violet Flame can transform doubts, fears and negative energy into positive thoughts and actions.

Fire was a key component in the evolution of mankind, bringing change and transformation to everyday activities, to life itself. Initially supplying light and heat that mankind could control and use, it became the focus of family, tribe or village. This central fire became the place of rites and ceremonies creating unity among the people. The fireplace or hearth has stood throughout history as an important aspect of any home. The Violet Flame combines that energy of unity and ceremony of the fire with its spiritual colour.

Fire is used for cleansing old unwanted energy, making way for new growth and has long been used by farmers at the end of harvest to return nutrients to the ground ready for seeds to be sown. Life will spring up again after forest fires. Fire is necessary to forge many things from glassware to tools and implements, demonstrating the destructive and creative elements of fire which are also within the Violet Flame.

Flames were often used for scrying, that ability to 'see' other potential futures by gazing into a naked flame. As it flickers and moves, it creates shapes and shadows that some can interpret.

Burnt at the stake

A client once told me that she had been experiencing flash-backs of being burnt at the stake as a witch in a previous incarnation. She said that the flames had burnt with shades of violet, purple and mauve which she remembered had made her feel unafraid, so she had wondered if this could have somehow been a life working with the Violet Flame, as she was so fascinated by it in this lifetime. I think this is highly likely as we do retain certain characteristics, traits and interests throughout many lifetimes. As the colour relates to transforma-tion, carrying energy from one state of being to another, the violet within the flames which carried her back into Spirit would have eased her passing without any fear.

She is still learning more about the Violet Flame and has now been able to forgive those who put her to death, understanding that their motives were fear and knowing that she took none of that with her as she returned to Spirit.

How does it work?

Every action starts with a thought

We have come to accept the power of thought; thought is energy; energy moves matter.

Whatever is the 'matter' in your life; you can move it or change it using the power of your thoughts. When those thoughts utilise the energy of the Violet Flame, the changes are more powerful and can be quite dramatic!

We feel and respond to the thoughts and intentions of others daily. Being loved creates a wonderful feeling; our energy swells and grows with the thoughts and intentions of the person who loves us. Likewise when we are not liked by someone, their thoughts can affect us in a very negative way, making us feel weak and vulnerable without even knowing why.

Our own thoughts affect us in exactly the same way! We can affect any situation by positive thought or by negative thought; it is a matter of choice. The Violet Flame will ensure the outcome is positive.

Be careful what you wish for

We have learnt that intent is the most important thought energy we can control and change at will, so when setting your intention think carefully about the outcome you wish to achieve and how you wish to achieve it, (for example: not at someone else's expense or suffering). Remember we do affect others by our thoughts as well our actions. Whatever situation we are using the Violet Flame for, if it involves other people we have to include them when setting our intent, stating that it will be for the Highest Good of all concerned.

Our ultimate aim is to reconnect with our Higher Self and become the entire spiritual being that we all are, living our lives in accordance with our soul's original plan, and to reunite with Source.

"I can't do that"
"Oh yes, you can!"

We are all made out of the same energy which is referred to as our 'Source'. That energy, like pure diamond white light, carries all the different vibrations or frequencies that we see as colour, all mixed together. Every one of us has Violet Light within our energy. If you like, we are all 'rainbow' beings, formed out of light energy, into a physical body. So just by tapping into that energy you already carry, using it every day, making it the strongest colour of light within you – that makes you Magic!

All you need is:

    the Desire or Intent to change,
    the Will to make it happen
    and the Violet Flame will do the rest.

CHAPTER 1

Summary

What is the Violet Flame, why is it violet, why is it a flame and how does it work?

♦ While in the past it was customary to invoke the Violet Flame by repeating decrees, the Elohim encourage us now to work with the Violet Flame in any way we choose.

♦ No 'attunements' are needed; the more you learn of the Violet Flame and the more you use it, incorporating it into your life, the more you can achieve.

♦ People react to the Violet Flame without knowing why.

♦ Violet is pink and blue combined – Love and Power, or Desire and Will. It is the highest vibration of light that we can see with the naked eye. It relates to our seventh or crown chakra beyond which our energy is spiritual or ethereal rather than physical.

♦ The Violet Flame reflects in our aura and can be seen by others.

♦ Flames, heat and fire have been used throughout the evolution of mankind for clearing, transformation, and in ceremonies and magic. These are also attributes of the Violet Flame.

♦ The Violet Flame works through the power of thought, intent, and will for the Highest Good.

♦ The Violet Flame cannot be used to bend another's will or control their freedom of choice, nor can it be used at some one else's cost.

♦ The Violet Flame is highly concentrated energy of Violet Light. It is the vibration of energy that creates change and transformation.

♦ Violet Light is within each one of us. Focus on and intensify that violet frequency of light and build it into the Violet Flame.

CHAPTER 2

BACKGROUND AND ATTRIBUTES

It helps to have some understanding of the Violet Flame, and to know how it has grown and evolved over thousands of years on Earth, yet is timeless beyond our knowledge. Its attributes or properties have also changed as the needs of mankind and civilisations have changed.

Where does it come from?

Because the Violet Flame is a Multi-Universal energy, not limited by the dimensions of Space or Time, it has no source, no beginning or end.

It is an energy that has been known of and used by many evolutions of mankind on Earth, throughout the Universe and through all dimensions. It once was an actual flame kept burning in the temples of ancient civilisations such as Atlantis and Lemuria and even further back long before any time we are aware of now. People would go to the Violet Flame temples for healing and to be cleansed of any negative energy which could cause dis-ease or illness. It was utilised by many ancient civilisations to enhance the growth of ideas and inspirations which enabled them to advance to a state of accomplishment that we are still in awe of today.

There are places within the many Universes which hold a concentration of the Violet Flame energy that we may draw on. One such place we refer to as The Violet Planet with its ruler Omri-Tas. On Earth, there are reservoirs of Violet Flame energy at the planet's core, and in the etheric realms above Europe. These can never be depleted or used up and we can draw on them at any time for any purpose that is for the Highest Good.

The Violet Flame is an energy that has been revived here on Earth again, expanding in the consciousness of mankind for us to evolve further. It has helped many to bring about changes in their lives, to transform negativity, to settle Karma, and to forgive. It is a wonderful versatile energy that has many applications and a huge variety of ways in which it can be used.

How the Violet Flame evolved

In ancient times it was known as the Violet Flame of Freedom, as that was seen as its main, all encompassing attribute. It was used to gain freedom from illness, fear and negativity.

Kuan Yin, Goddess of Mercy throughout the Far East, was revered as being a Guardian of the Violet Flame for two thousand years. So her 'Mercy Flame' combined with the 'Freedom Flame' when she presided over the Violet Ray of Light. Eventually in the 1700s she passed the administration of the Violet Ray over to St. Germain and his Lady Portia. These are the Ascended Masters who are still Guardians and Directors of the Violet Flame to this day. Lady Portia represents Justice and is often depicted with the scales of justice and the sword of truth, or with the 'Justice Flame'.

The Violet Flame was then often portrayed as a triple flame, incorporating Freedom, Mercy, and Justice; the freedom from all ills and negativity, the mercy of compassionate understanding, and the justice of balance and equality.

As the Violet Flame has grown and evolved, many more spiritual beings from other realms, such as Archangel Zadkiel,

Merlin, and the Elohim, have become associated with it too, so now it encompasses the added qualities of Forgiveness, Transmutation, Sacred Ceremony, and Magic! *

*All these Guardians and Directors of the Violet Flame and their teachings feature in my second book: 'A Spiritual Guide to the Violet Flame'.

What does the Violet Flame do?

The Violet Flame now has seven main attributes:

- *Freedom*...... from dis-ease, illness, and low or base energy
- *Mercy*......... compassionate understanding without judgement
- *Justice*........ balance, equality, and settlement of karmic debts
- *Forgiveness*.. of self and others for any hurt and suffering
- *Transmutation*... of negativity
  – our own, environmental, and planetary
- *Sacred Ceremony*... rites of passage
  – from one state of being to another
- *Magic*......... creating a sudden transmutation of energy

Energy medicine

Freedom from dis-ease

Dis-ease can cause disease, or illness. Change to being at-ease and your well-being will increase. The Violet Flame will transmute blocked energy within the physical body and the energy body or aura that can cause dis-ease. The mental and emotional states too can be cleared and rebalanced with the Violet Flame.

I believe. dis-ease occurs when the body is vibrating at a different rate from the Higher Self. The Violet Flame restores the natural resonance between the two, linking through the Higher Self to Guides, Guardians, and all other Light Beings.

To me, the Violet Flame has become my greatest medicine! I rarely even get a cold, for at the first signs of a dry throat or that tickle in my nose that starts to feel hot, I re-ignite the Violet Flame at my heart and visualise a little Violet Flame like a cartoon character and set it to seek out the virus and smother it. I imagine the little flame surrounding the virus and transmuting it totally, virtually cuddling it to death! It certainly works for me.

Clearly it won't cure all illnesses, for some things we have chosen to experience this lifetime; some accidents do happen and they provide opportunities to learn other lessons, but I am sure I will not learn anything more from just another cold. I do however take it as a warning to slow down, boost my immune system or just focus my attention back onto myself for a while. When such a time occurs, I make sure I have a 'treat' or some 'me time', as this is what we do when we have a cold. So I react consciously to the lesson without having to experience the cold, and the Violet Flame is the method or tool I use.

Who are we to judge?

Mercy, Justice, and Forgiveness for emotional balance

By using the Violet Flame at times of trauma or emotional upset, the feelings of frustration, anger, and the desire for revenge can be tempered with mercy and bring understanding and compassion which can then lead to forgiveness. This creates the balance of true justice stopping the destructive energy from consuming or damaging you and allowing the situation or person to heal. This can be done in retrospect and works very well on painful memories, and scars we so often carry from past experiences. It is often good to remember that we learn the most from the hardest lessons.

The Violet Flame has changed my perception of other people and enabled me to separate the person from their behaviour. Behaviour is learned, and that is the issue to be judged, not the soul. Each person here on Earth is on their own soul's journey, learning different lessons at vastly different rates, and some have chosen very hard lessons to learn from!

I am also reminded of those from our soul group: parents, siblings, teachers, friends and partners, who play such a big part in our lives. Imagine sitting with them all in a large circle in the spirit realms before incarnating on Earth to live another lifetime. As each soul chooses their experiences and lessons to be learned, the members of the soul group volunteer to play different parts in each other's lives according to their own plans. Who would volunteer to cause heartache, misery, or pain? No one wants to be the 'bad guy' so why would we do that to each other if not out of love and understanding? We learn the most from the hardest lessons, so who would provide those hard lessons? Only those who love us enough to care about our soul's growth.

Seeing the hurt and pain I have experienced at times in my own life, through the attributes of Mercy and Justice within the Violet Flame, has enabled me to forgive those who have hurt me. This has been one of the most liberating aspects of the Violet Flame for me, taking away all bitterness and emotional scars.

Paying back the IOU's

Justice to settle karmic debts

A large part of what we refer to as 'Justice' involves the balancing or settlement of karma. There are different aspects to this issue:

♦ The karmic 'debts' we owe each other throughout many life times – those pre-agreed interactions with our soul group and with others we meet on our life's journey. The Violet Flame will help to balance these debts so that they cancel each other out – like swings and roundabouts.

♦ The karmic debt we owe our soul or Higher Self to experi ence life to the fullest, to learn from each experience without repetition of our actions. (Think of 'Groundhog Day' – repeating each day over and over again until we get it right!) So by reacting to each experience differently we eventually respond in the correct way in order to move on. Human beings though by nature are creatures of habit, and we do respond to situations the same way time after time. The Violet Flame can help to change this pattern so that we can release the karmic debt to our souls.

♦ Earth's karma is all past damage, trauma, and abuse that we have caused, as well as the havoc which natural disasters have caused to all life forms. The Violet Flame can help our planet transform back to a state of peace, balance, harmony, and freedom.

It is only when all Karma is settled and balanced that we can be free.

Change of mind

Transmutation of negative thoughts for mental ease

The Violet Flame can transform or transmute negative doubts, fears, pessimism, low self-esteem and unnecessary anxiety.

These are traits that we all have in varying degrees; it is when they become imbalanced or take over our lives that problems can occur. To restore the balance, the Violet Flame can remove blockages and change those negative patterns of behaviour, helping us to see a situation as it really is, creating a more positive outcome.

My sister used to complain that I was such a pessimist. As we grew up I would always think the worst of every situation, imagining 'what if?' and expecting failure and disappointments. She, in contrast, was a total optimist, always cheerful, and saw the positive side to everything. We got on really well! She was my idol! Sadly it wasn't until after she passed away that I discovered the Violet Flame and transmuted all my negativity!

People who know me now, know me as optimistic and may find it incredible that I used to be so different.

Have a clear out

Transmutation of negative environmental energy

You know when you walk into a building or room and your energy drains, you suddenly feel tired, fed up or uncomfortable? You may well be responding subconsciously to negative energy within the place. All people affect their environment. Negative thoughts, attitudes, confrontations or arguments create energy that can affect the atmosphere or ambience anywhere. This energy can build up over a long period of time until many will sense the 'heavy atmosphere'. Negativity can also come from the land itself, such as fault lines or negative ley lines and geopathic stress within the Earth.

Transmuting negative energy with the Violet Flame will create a more positive environment in which to live or work.

The Violet Flame is also a wonderful tool for clearing crystals. As crystals absorb and transmit energy it is advisable to cleanse them when you first buy them or before and after use in healing treatments or meditations to remove any negativity.

You can clear the energy of just about anything and anywhere with the Violet Flame – it will transmute all negative energy, raising the vibration of wherever you go, and whatever you do.

Rites of passage

Sacred Ceremony to enhance our spiritual connection

The Violet Flame has long been used in spiritual ceremonies, celebrations, rites of passage and times of transition. Throughout history the colours purple and deep violet have been used to stand for pomp and ceremony, victory, and recognition of status. Even in religious ceremonies, purple was traditionally the colour of sacred rites, including the robes worn by priests, and it was the colour of the lining of coffins for royalty. Purple cloaks were worn by triumphant Roman Generals and it was even one of the predominant colours chosen by the Suffragettes; all heralding change and victory, ceremony and sacred passage.

The Violet Flame provides the energy to make the change from one state of being to another as smooth as possible. A violet glow has often been reported in the "tunnel of light" experienced in near death episodes and also when a soul departs from this life or a baby is born in to it. The energy of the Violet Flame acts as a gateway or passage between physical and spiritual realms.

The Violet Flame is the energy that connects the physical 'you' with the spiritual 'you' or your Higher Self. It is all too easy to become entrenched in this materialistic world that is focused on work and money, forgetting that we are primarily spiritual beings who have chosen to live in a physical body. Through the Violet Flame that connection can be restored or enhanced, giving you understanding of who you truly are, your soul' journey and your life's purpose.

"Just like that!"

– Tommy Cooper

It's just Magic!

When enough Violet Flame energy has been built up the transformation can be very quick, resulting in what is perceived as a miracle or magic. As you work more and more with its energy, you will find that it strengthens and quickens within you until you feel that anything is possible – you are magic – so be careful what you wish for!

There have been times in the past when there was so much fear in the world that knowledge of the Violet Flame was limited to those who were able to fully understand and respect it, who were trained in its use, and desired to create change for the Highest Good. These were frequently monks and devout people who held purity in their hearts to ease the suffering of others. They were known as great philosophers and physicians in their time.

King Arthur's adviser Merlin, (said to be an incarnation of St. Germain who is one of the Guardians of the Violet Flame) created such sudden changes that they were seen as magic through people's lack of understanding of the power of the Violet Flame energy. Merlin is often referred to as a great Alchemist because of his ability to change, or alter the state of matter and the Alchemists are most remembered for their attempts to turn base metal, usually lead, into gold.

Don't try this at home! The Violet Flame IS magic, but not for material gain!

However the spiritual application of Alchemy is to transmute mankind's base desires and instincts into the higher vibrations of energy and stronger connections to Spirit. In effect, the Violet Flame turns our dense energy (like the lead) into 'spiritual gold'. If each person lives their life in accordance with their divine self, acknowledging their own power and strength to co-create the world we all want – it will happen – as if by magic!

CHAPTER 2

Summary

Where does the Violet Flame come from, how has it evolved and what does it do?

- The Violet Flame is multi-dimensional, multi-universal energy utilised by ancient civilisations on Earth such as Lemuria and Atlantis.

- The highest concentration of Violet Flame energy is on The Violet Planet, ruled over by Omri-Tas, but there are reservoirs on Earth at the planet's core and in the etheric layer over central Europe.

- Kuan Yin presided over the entire Violet Ray of Light for 2,000 years then handed over to St. Germain and Lady Portia who are the current Guardians of the Violet Ray and therefore the Violet Flame also.

- Originally known as the Violet Flame of Freedom, Kuan Yin added her 'Mercy Flame', and then Lady Portia added her 'Justice Flame'. It then became known as a threefold flame.

- The Violet Flame now has seven main attributes:

Freedom............ from dis-ease, illness and low or base energy
Mercy.............. compassionate understanding without judgement
Justice............. balance, equality, and settlement of karmic debts
Forgiveness...... of self and others for any hurt and suffering
Transmutation... of negativity – our own, environmental, and planetary
Sacred Ceremony rites of passage from one state of being to another
Magic.............. creating a sudden transmutation of energy

CHAPTER 3

PREPARING TO WORK WITH THE VIOLET FLAME

Get ready...

In order to integrate and work with any higher vibrational frequencies of energy such as the Violet Flame, preparation is not only very important but absolutely essential. Only then will you feel your energy field quicken, your levels of awareness rise, and the Violet Flame energy will flow freely through and around you.

There are several ways to prepare. It is at this stage that you are setting your intent, making it known to your own personal Guides and the Guardians of the Violet Flame that you will be working with this energy. This does not have to be done through meditation, so do not be put off by that suggestion if you have not tried it before. You may choose to prepare simply by closing your eyes and paying attention to breathing slowly and deeply until you feel calm and all other thoughts have gone from your mind, or you may find repeating a mantra or affirmation works better for you.

It is important that you are sitting comfortably and quietly where you will not be disturbed, so unplug the phone, play some soft background music if that helps you to focus, and light a candle or incense if that is your preference. Once you have set your intent and followed whichever of the methods you feel are right for you, the preparation will become quicker, more automatic, and with time you may find that any of the following exercises can be integrated into your daily routine, for example in the shower or even when cleaning your teeth!

By then you will feel the Violet Flame is always just a thought away, the energy builds quicker and becomes stronger and stronger.

Get set...

Grounding

It is first essential to anchor your energy into the Earth to stabilise you and stop you feeling light-headed. This is often referred to as 'grounding'.

This can be achieved through the visualisation of roots extending from the soles of your feet down deep into the ground and connecting to the Earth's core, or by repeating a mantra or affirmation to set your intent to be grounded.

Remember it is the power of thought that produces the action.

Visualisation:

 "Sit somewhere comfortable and take three deep breaths. As you breathe out feel your physical body relax, drop your shoulders, let your muscles soften and your limbs become heavy. Feel the weight of your hands in your lap, your own weight on the seat and your feet firmly on the floor.

Take your attention down to the soles of your feet and imagine strong white roots growing from them, pushing down through the floor, twisting and entwining around each other, blending into one strong tap root. Your root pushes down through the foundations of the building. Beneath the foundations on the surface of the soil is a bright circle of light, spinning clockwise. It spins at a smooth regular speed, forming a perfect open circle. Your root drops through its centre and enters the earth.

With every breath out, feel that root pushing down through soft layers of rock, through limestone and clay, sinking down through underground water, finding its way through cracks and fissures in the harder layers of rock, passing through caves and caverns, layers of minerals and crystals, descending deeper and deeper down through the heat of the molten lava; the liquefied rock and metal that swirls around the Earths core. Your root passes through, being pulled by the magnetic energy of the iron rock at the centre. Feel it strike the rock and attach there, held strongly and securely by the magnetic energy.

As you breathe in, draw that energy of the Earth back up through your root, feel the warmth rising within it through all the layers of rock, water and soil. Feel the strength of your connection to the Earth's core as it rises through your feet and your legs, drawing up into your physical body. Let your breath expand with the Earth's energy; feel grounded and secure here.

Whenever you are ready you can open your eyes."

With practice, this becomes quicker and quicker.

Affirmation:

 Another option is to take three deep breaths and as you breathe out repeat any phrase that you feel appropriate to ground yourself for example:

"My roots connect me to the heart of Mother Earth – I am grounded".

Go...

Ignite the Spark!

You already carry the energy of Violet Light within you; it is part of the spectrum of light that all life forms are created from. The next step is to focus on the part of your energy that is Violet Light, and bring it all to your heart centre either by visualisation, mantra or affirmation to set the intent. Ask for the Violet Flame energy from Universal Source to enter your crown chakra and descend to strengthen the Violet Light at your heart, increasing the concentration until it ignites a spark of the Violet Flame within you.

Visualisation:

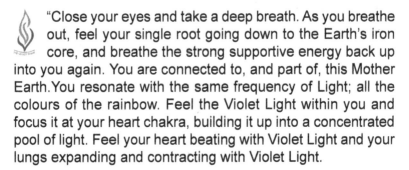 "Close your eyes and take a deep breath. As you breathe out, feel your single root going down to the Earth's iron core, and breathe the strong supportive energy back up into you again. You are connected to, and part of, this Mother Earth. You resonate with the same frequency of Light; all the colours of the rainbow. Feel the Violet Light within you and focus it at your heart chakra, building it up into a concentrated pool of light. Feel your heart beating with Violet Light and your lungs expanding and contracting with Violet Light.

Ask for the multidimensional energy of the Violet Flame to enhance that vibration within you and imagine a thin stream of Violet Light like a laser beam descending down from above, through your crown chakra. Feel it pass down through the centre of your head, your neck, and your chest, stopping at your heart chakra where it combines with your own Violet Light, becoming so intense that it sparks into a flame.

You feel the Violet Flame flicker and grow as your heart chakra expands with Violet Light and the glow of the Flame begins to spread out, filling your rib cage and your chest. It spreads across your shoulders, easing any tension, soothing away any stiffness as it flows down your spine and down your arms to the tips of your fingers. The energy of the Violet Flame builds up through your neck and in to your head. Feel it flowing along your jaw through your sinuses, and the space behind your eyes; soothing your mind, easing your thoughts, transmuting any negative doubts and fears. The glow of the Violet Flame in your heart also spreads down through all the organs of your body, neutralising any toxins, empowering them to work at their best. It spreads through your muscles and bones to the central nervous system running down your spine, so all the nerves in your entire body enhance your physical senses of sight, sound, touch, smell, and taste.

Feel the Violet Light releasing any tension through your hips, flowing down your legs, relaxing and softening the muscles, easing around your knees and ankles all the way down to your feet and the tips of your toes. Your body is filled with Violet Light. All blockages of energy have dissipated and all negativity has gone. You feel clear, pure and light.

Open your chakras in front of you and at your back releasing the Violet Light out into your aura. As it spreads through your aura, all negativity and energy blocks held there disappear as they are transmuted to positive energy. You can breathe in Violet Light and breathe out Violet Light for it flows through you and surrounds you. Imagine a shiny layer of golden light around the outer edge of your aura, protecting and shielding your entire being. You are transformed into a Being of Violet Light, part of the highest vibrational frequency of light here on Earth. You are at One with the Universe, existing in all dimensions throughout all time. You experience ultimate peace and unconditional love.

When you are ready, let your breath deepen as your conscious mind returns your awareness to your surroundings here and now. Feel your feet on the floor and your strong root still connecting you to the centre of the Earth and open your eyes."

This can be done at any time to clear your physical self and extended energy field (aura), transmuting any negativity into positive energy in preparation for your work with the Violet Flame. Once you have acknowledged and lit the spark of Violet Flame at your heart, it is with you always and whenever you feel the need you can refocus your attention on that spark and reignite it into a flame. Feel it come to life again and its glow spread through you. Remember to keep a protective shield around the outside of your aura to maintain the energy and stop any negative influences affecting it.

Mantra or Affirmation:

 If you are not comfortable with meditation or visualisation, read the following slowly, out loud, pausing at the end of each line to feel the words taking effect.

"I accept the Violet Flame into my heart,
Its glow spreads throughout my entire body,
I am filled with Violet Light.

All aches, pains, and tiredness are washed away by
     the Violet Light.
All doubts, fears, and life's limitations disappear into
     the Violet Light.
I am at peace as the Violet Light shines through me,
     filling my entire energy body.

I breathe in Violet Light,
I breathe out Violet Light.

I live my life in the Light of the Violet Flame,
I AM Freedom, Mercy, and Justice,
And the Flame burns forever in my heart."

Whilst proof-reading and editing this book, Jennifer Sheldon was inspired to write her own, poetic version. She has given me permission to share this:

> "I light again the Violet Flame.
> I start the violet spark that shelters at my heart,
> That fans violet,
> Dances violet,
> Flames violet
> To the edge of the shimmering golden shield.
> Within is warm, cleansed, transformed.
> I am the Violet Flame."

CHAPTER 3

Summary

Preparing to work with the Violet Flame

◆ Make your intent to work with the Violet Flame known to your own Guides, and the Guardians of the Violet Flame.

◆ The Violet Flame is only a thought away. With practice you will feel the energy is instantly accessible.

◆ When working with higher vibrations of energy such as the Violet Flame, it is vital to ground yourself, creating your own anchor from which to feel and be both stable and secure.

◆ To ignite the Violet Flame within your heart chakra use visualisation, a mantra or affirmation.

◆ It is important to protect the outer layer of your aura with gold light when your energy field is filled with Violet Flame.

◆ Once you have ignited the Violet Flame at your heart chakra, it remains alight there forever.

CHAPTER 4

HERE'S HOW...

Ways to work with the Violet Flame

Many civilisations over thousands of years have utilised the Violet Flame. We have grown up and evolved with it, adapting the ways we use it, work with it, and share it. In these times of immense potential for change, there is no limit to the methods we can use to call upon the energy that will help those changes happen. We can let our imagination work with the Violet Flame, in whatever way feels right for us individually, to invoke the energy to manifest a life and world of positivity and love. That can be using visualisation and meditation, or with the voice – talking, chanting or singing, or through art, music, dance, poetry, or by carrying out rites and ceremonies.

I wholeheartedly believe it is the power of thought, honest intent, and the Violet Flame that will create 'Heaven on Earth'. How each individual achieves that is of no matter. The more people who dance in the Violet Flame, whether formal or freestyle, focusing their energy, the quicker it will happen. The objective is the same however we get there.

People have expressed their criticism of the state of our world, sharing their opinions, views, and ideals. The image of a more perfect world has formed in many people's hearts and minds. The desire and will for change has been gathering momentum, with thoughts and perceptions becoming clearer and more focused. Now we can act on those ideals and create the life and the world that we want to live in, and the best tool we have is undoubtedly the energy of the Violet Flame.

"Logic will take you from A to B
Imagination will take you everywhere"
— Albert Einstein

Use your imagination!

Visualisation and Meditation

This is one of the most effective ways to use the Violet Flame
for those who are visual and comfortable meditating. Meditating stimulates the connection with your Higher Self and the
spiritual realms enabling you to draw more of the Violet Flame
energy through your crown chakra and filling your entire being.

(For those of you who do not regularly meditate, do not be put
off trying this method. Visualisation is just another word used
to describe using your imagination, creating an image in your
mind. Meditation is focusing on that image and allowing it to
develop.)

Before you meditate remember to ground yourself first by
sending roots down to the centre of the earth. (This preparation
is described in Chapter 3 under 'Get Set....')

"After you have grounded yourself, sit quietly, close your
eyes and imagine you are standing in front of a mirror.
Look at your reflection closely, note what you are wearing
– it does not have to be what you put on that morning! Imagine
what background you can see in the mirror – outside with fields
and trees?...in a forest perhaps?...by the sea?...or at home
by a warm fire?...in a study surrounded by books? Let your
imagination fill in the background.

Now visualise a fine violet mist swirling around your image in
the mirror, blocking out the background, 'see' yourself smiling,
happy and healthy, looking radiant and glowing through the

violet mist. As the mist dissolves and you can see the background again, you may find it has changed; you are not where you thought you were. Just see that wherever you are, wherever you go, you are happy, healthy, and glowing with a Violet Light.

Take a deep breath in as you become aware again of the chair you are sitting in, the reality of the room around you, and open your eyes whenever you are ready".

How do you feel now? Are you still smiling? Remember the feeling as you go through the day and week ahead.

Suppose you could bring about a change to any situation just by 'imagining' it. For your health, you could meditate on 'seeing' yourself in the mirror but able to see inside your body, where there is any injury, inflammation or infection. Visualise the Violet Flame energy as a mist going to the part of your body that is affected. Doing this regularly assists the body's natural healing ability. Remember it is not 'a quick fix' so keep practising.

As you become more at ease with meditation, you can visualise any situation that you would wish to change, whether it is from the past, present or future. For example: a time when you were angry and later regretted the words you said. Go through a replay of the incident in your mind – just like we can now do with the television – see it happen just as you remember it, but this time with the Violet Flame energy built up within you, glowing all around you and encompassing anyone who heard your anger. Keep the details as sharp in your mind as you can but as if you are seeing it through a violet filter. Repeat the visualisation whenever you can until you feel the anger has transmuted to meaningless words that can then be laughed at by all parties. Imagine a humorous response and laughter within the Violet Light.

Those who had been involved may well respond to this without knowing why, and thereafter forgiveness is easier to seek and to be given.

For any future occurrence, set the intention to project the Violet Flame to that time and imagine it occurring within the glow of Violet Light. Visualise all going smoothly, the best possible outcome for all concerned, Violet Flames flickering over any doubts and fears, transmuting the negativity. Recall the feeling of happiness and radiance that you saw in the mirror and imagine that feeling spreading through the entire event.

There is no limit!

Violet Flame Spheres

 Imagine a 'water bomb' but filled with Violet Flame energy dropping on an area or a person and exploding as 'water bombs' do, releasing a mist of Violet Light to spread wherever it is needed for the Highest Good. This method can have an immediate effect, so use it carefully! For these to drop, ask Omri-Tas, the ruler of the Violet Planet, to send Violet Flame Spheres to wherever it is needed. Do not hesitate to ask for his help for you personally or for the planet as a whole. I imagine him as incredibly tall and powerful in long violet robes, surrounded by a Violet Light that fills my view. Rather than throwing the spheres like I would imagine Zeus or Thor would throw thunderbolts, I see him just opening his out-stretched hands and simply letting them roll off and drop.

Drop anchor!

Anchor the Violet Flame to a certain place

 To set a Violet Flame anchor, stand at the central spot of the place you wish to set a flame to burn. Build up the intensity of Violet Light at your heart chakra igniting your own flame and feel its glow expand throughout your body. Imagine that you are standing in a dish or recess set into the floor and take in a deep breath; as you breathe out let the intensity of the Violet Light sink down to your feet. Feel a flame ignite there, burning within the dish or recess around your feet and simply step out of it leaving the Violet Flame to burn there. Set the intent that its glow will have the greatest effect for the Highest Good. Whenever you pass that spot again, imagine the Violet Flame still alight and glowing there. No one else need know if you feel it would not be understood or accepted; the energy is simply there if it is needed. This can be done in a building that needs clearing, in your own home, out in nature – absolutely anywhere, just by thinking it, imagining it and setting the intent. Animals and the natural world are familiar with it and will benefit from it; people will respond without knowing why.

What did you say?

Decrees, mantras and affirmations

For those who are not visual, the repetition of Decrees, Mantras, and Affirmations will work just as well. Remember it is the intent that is important!

This goes back to ancient times when sacred knowledge and symbols were taught and used by the students through repetition of the spoken word, like the mantras we still use. These were passed on, generation to generation, and so had to be learnt by repetition. The energy builds up slowly in the rhythm of repetition and as the words sink into your subconscious their energy is embedded within you.

If you feel drawn to using this method, there are Violet Flame decrees in books and on the internet that you can use, or do have a bit of fun writing your own. The Guardians and Directors of the Violet Flame urge us to be creative with methods of invoking the energy, so whichever way you choose if it is done from the heart, with pure intent, there are no rules.

Decrees tend to be a couple of lines that rhyme.
For example:

"I am a being of Violet Fire
            - Raising my vibration ever higher"

"I invoke the Flame of the Violet Ray
        - To cleanse and protect me every day."

"I live my life in the Violet Ray
        - Its Light surrounds me every day."

Mantras are statements of fact.
For example:

"The Violet Flame transforms our world to a state
      of pure love."

"Om Mani Padme Hum"

This mantra of Kuan Yin, can be interpreted in several ways. 'Hail the jewel in the Lotus' or 'The jewel of the mind has reached the Lotus of the heart'. (Kuan Yin is still very much associated with the Violet Flame.)

Affirmations are personal.
For example:

"I am transformed within the Violet Flame.
      I am the Violet Flame."

"I hold the Violet Flame sacred within my heart;
its Light shines through me."

The nice thing about mantras and affirmations, for the non-poets, is that you don't have to make them rhyme, and often the simpler they are the better! Do have fun writing your own to use, the energy you put into the creation of any decree, mantra, or affirmation will strengthen the outcome and be more personal to you.

Violet Flame decrees, mantras or affirmations should be repeated in multiples of 3 or 7, so say, chant or sing them either to yourself or out loud until you feel the energy build up.

The reason for repeating them in multiples of 3 or 7 is because:
• 3 refers to the triple flame of Freedom, Mercy and Justice as it was in ancient times.
• 7 refers to all seven attributes the Flame now carries which are: Freedom, Mercy, Justice, Forgiveness, Transmutation Sacred Ceremony, and Magic.

"Writing... is a mirror made of words"
– Aberjhani

Writing to release

Writing things down can enable you to reflect on exactly what it is you wish to change, which negative experiences need to be released and allow emotional pain to heal.

Try to be totally honest, and hold the purest intent to heal. It is important that this is done with love. To invoke the Violet Flame energy of transformation in this method you may want to write on violet coloured paper, use a violet pen or even draw violet coloured flames over what you have written. The writing also then becomes visual as you see the colour violet transforming the energy of your words. This can be kept in a violet coloured box or file until you feel the issue is cleared or settled – providing that only you have access to it!

A word of warning: anything you write may be read by the very person you may have written about, so take this into consideration. The writing can be kept by someone you trust, it can be burnt as soon as you have written it or any issues can be written as a story in the third person, changing any names. This does not alter your intent or the outcome of transmuting the energy of it.

At any time it can be burned in the flame of a violet candle, one that is violet all the way through, not just dipped in colour. Only do this outside in the open air where you can see the smoke rise taking the energy with it. Hold your letter or note with long tweezers preferably over a cast iron pot or old saucepan that is no longer used. This saves burning the ground or letting the energy of what you are releasing go into the Earth. You can also be sure that it has completely burned and extinguished! Visualise the smoke as violet as it rises into the air.

It is often worth it quite some time to later to think of rewriting it, just to see how your feelings have changed.

Writing to manifest

 I have found this very helpful when clearing past upset or trauma, but this method can also be used to manifest or to create a desired outcome if it is for the Highest Good.

Think carefully about what you wish for or you may achieve it in a way that was not intended. Please bear in mind it will only work for the Highest Good and is neither for gaining riches in the physical world, nor is it for bending someone else's will to yours. The Violet Flame will transmute the energy of any blockages that stand in the way, for example your own doubts and fears, so in this way can be used for the future and not just the past.

Try to be realistic in your goals and aims for what you wish to happen. Write honestly and from your heart the scenario or occurrence you are focusing on. For example, passing an exam will only happen if you have also worked and revised for it! Write down the things that you may feel could hold you back, such as nerves or poor health. When all these details are surrounded with the Violet Flame by whatever method you use, the outcome will always be for the Highest Good.

Seeing the truth

To test this for yourself, you can write down all that you understand or have been told about a situation. Hold the paper in your hands or put it into a purple or violet coloured plastic document wallet, one that you can see through, close your eyes and visualise or repeat a mantra or affirmation to build the Violet Flame energy within you. Feel the Violet Light of it expanding through you and out into your aura, encompassing and seeping through the paper or wallet in your hands. Set the intent that the Violet Flame will transmute all distortions leaving only the truth visible. The power of your mind in setting that intent ensures that is what your eyes will automatically be drawn to. Open your eyes and see the words or parts that are true. Each time you do this your eyes will be drawn to just the truth, all else will be ignored or not even noticed.

I met Heather through my own business, 'Amethyst', and she told me that after learning of this application of the Violet Flame, she always used it in her own business, becoming very astute and gaining a reputation for the ability to see the truth. I heard her staff say that it was pointless trying to get away with anything for she always seemed to know, and one of her suppliers commented that she drove a hard bargain!

"Creativity is just connecting things in a different way"
– Steve Jobs

Being creative

 There is no limit to creativity, so do use your imagination. If you are very visual and like playing around with computer images, then it can be satisfying to deal with issues in this way – either reorganising photographs, editing them with a violet tint, even giving a file a new title such as: 'Things to transmute in the Violet Flame'. Feel the energy of the Violet Flame going to all the situations, people or places that you put into your file.

If you have imaging software – please no beards, moustaches, glasses, horns or other distortions to those who may have offended you, however tempting and amusing it may seem at the time! Use it for the Highest Good and keep your focus on the Flame!

Drawing and painting

 Much passion and emotion can be expressed in drawing, painting and even just in random doodles. Focus on a situation or issue that you wish to alter in any way: letting go, changing perceptions, building the energy of some future occurrence. Pick up some crayons or paint and give it a go. The expectation is not to create a masterpiece, you don't have to have any artistic ability; it is simply your own expression of your feelings. You can then keep or burn it as you wish, but as it is an abstract representation it may be safer to keep than the written word.

You may find symbols such as the Lemniscate, (the figure of eight on its side which is the symbol of infinity), very pleasing and satisfying to draw or doodle in violet. This carries the energy of the Violet Flame throughout time, reaching back into the past, and forward to the future. Think about what you might like to write in the 'loops' of the symbol for the energy to flow endlessly around. You can create any pattern of energy, or mandala, with violet, mauve and purple colours holding the intent of the Violet Flame in your mind and write a dedication over it or on the back, to send the Violet Flame to some person, place or purpose.

Do we have to redecorate?

Creating a sacred space

Sometimes it is nice to display objects together creating a place to focus, where you can set and hold the intent of working with the Violet Flame. Traditionally people have set up private altars and created sacred spaces within their homes or communities not just with religious intent but as a way of outwardly expressing what is important to them. Likewise people display collections of items that have a personal significance for no particular reason other than a hobby or interest.

Creating an altar or sacred space for the Violet Flame is simple. You can put a collection of items on a small table or window ledge, or anywhere convenient within your home. Just a few violet or purple items that appeal to you, a cloth or cushion, violet crystals, candles, flowers, or perhaps pictures of any of the Spirit Guides and Guardians associated with the Violet Flame starts to build the energy in that place. If this is impractical an alternative is to keep some of these items in a box, accessible only to you to bring out whenever you wish to focus on the Violet Flame.

At any time you can add to your collection: any photos, mementos, people's names written down or items that link to them, perhaps postcards or pictures of places that you would like to send the Violet Flame to. Just set your intent on a regular basis either by repeating decrees or mantras, visualisation, or by asking the Guides and Guardians to direct the Violet Flame energy to all who are represented there. Be careful not to display anything personal that you have written that you would not wish others to see.

It's crystal clear!

Using Crystals

Crystals have been used in healing for thousands of years throughout many cultures and civilisations. All crystals have their own specific attributes and their own vibrational frequency. They interact with the vibrational frequency, or energy, of our bodies and all living organisms. Their healing properties have been accepted for thousands of years without scientific proof, as part of a much more natural approach to health. Interest in working with crystals has grown as scientific research uncovers details that improve our understanding of how crystals work. They can balance, alter, regulate, enhance and energise on very many levels.

Quartz crystal is widely used in modern technology, in computers, clocks and watches for its piezoelectric properties. Quartz and garnet are both incorporated in radio transmitters and receivers as part of the mechanism that transforms and amplifies sound waves. Crystals are known to have transformational qualities. In crystals that carry the energy of the Violet Flame, those transformational qualities are even more intense.

Crystals form deep inside the Earth and even after they have been removed, cut and/or polished they continue to hold that connection. They therefore act as an anchor for other energies that vibrate at a higher frequency such as the Violet Flame. Many crystals carry the energy of the Violet Flame. Some of the more commonly known and readily available examples of these are:

Amethyst – for good all round healing, clearing old habits, headaches and nerves. Soothing and calming.

Ametrine – for clearing the mind, enabling decision making, overcoming fears and procrastination. Empowering and inspiring.

Charoite – for bringing one's own negativity to the surface in order to be cleared and protecting from other's negativity, strengthening sense of purpose and find ing your soul's path.

Iolite – for healing old wounds, for enhancing creativity, meditation and astral travel, encouraging positivity and clear perspective.

Lepidolite– for emotional healing, uplifting mood, bringing hope and support, lessening despair and even nightmares.

Purple Fluorite – for focus, clarity, and cutting through 'mind-chatter', sharpening psychic abilities, seeing the truth and eliminating confusion.

Purpurite – for purification, insight and enriching dreams, giving courage to explore and freedom from anxiety.

Stichtite – for releasing stubbornness and shyness, heightening love of life, links to Spirit, and joyful aware-ess. It soothes the nerves and energises the heart.

Sugilite – for forgiveness, alleviating guilt and destructive emotions, realising dreams and possibilities. For grounding, and protection while exploring other realms.

These are just a few of their individual attributes and healing properties, all of which are enhanced by their connection to the transformational energy of the Violet Flame.

You can place them anywhere around your home; more specifically you can place them on your altar or within your sacred space. You may like to place a Violet Flame crystal each side of your front door so as people enter, any negativity will be transmuted and your home will remain clear. Another possibility would be to place them around your bed or beneath your pillow to bring the attributes of the Violet Flame to you whilst you sleep, in fact anywhere that you are drawn to place them – be guided by your intuition.

It is also lovely to wear jewellery made with any of these crystals. Amethyst is very popular and easy to obtain.

Create a crystal mandala

This is a quick and easy method of sending the energy to somewhere or someone. A mandala is simply a pattern that creates energy to carry a specific intent. Using violet or purple coloured crystal tumble stones, place them in any pattern that you like, over the written name or photo of someone, a place or situation. This will carry a steady stream of Violet Flame energy to the focus of the mandala.

Cleansing crystals

The Violet Flame will cleanse any crystal, clearing it of whatever energy it may have absorbed from other people or situations. Some suggested ways of doing this are:

◆ Visualise a thin beam of Violet Light entering into the centre of any crystal, sparking in to a flame with its glow expanding out through the crystal's surface.

◆ Alternatively you could imagine a Violet Flame spark into life in the palms of your hands and hold the crystal bathing it in the Violet Light, until you intuitively feel it has been cleansed.

◆ You could hold it and silently repeat a mantra, or simply: "I cleanse this crystal in the Violet Flame". Imagine it surrounded by Violet Flames. Remember it is the intent that carries the energy.

This is why a bed or cave of Amethyst is so often recommended to cleanse and heal other crystals.

It's not all Lavender and Violets

Aura sprays & incense

There are several aura sprays and a variety of incense on the market, some now produced specifically to invoke the Violet Flame energy and some do carry that name. Aroma is very personal, like perfume, so choose carefully because the smell of a spray or incense burning can enhance anything that you do if it resonates with you in a harmonious way. Aura sprays are useful for clearing the energy of any space or room as well as your own personal energy, raising the vibration to that of the level of the Violet Flame if that is its specified purpose.

Personally, I find the Violet Flame Aura Sprays made by Samantha Belara Logan-Hochadel of 'Fulfilled Wishes' the best with an aroma, as they really capture the essence of the Violet Flame. Sam worked with the energy of St. Germain, asking for his help and advice to create these Aura Sprays, channelling the ingredients directly from him, so they contain something of his energy vibration too! The blend includes white, blue and pink Lotus flowers and now essences of some of the Violet Flame crystals too.

It is also possible to buy Crystal Essence Sprays that have no aroma at all but are made using only the energy of Violet Flame crystals. They are pure energy sprays, very powerful and effective for clearing negative energy. As they have no aroma they do not clash with perfume so can be used at any time within your aura, and can be used unobtrusively in your home or workplace. Of those that I have tried, I would recommend Jeni Powell's 'Crystal Balance' sprays. Jeni was influenced by a connection with Master Rakoczy, the Ascended Master who directed the Violet Flame to safe-keeping at the demise of Atlantis. He gave her the knowledge in meditation to make this aura spray, told her that its purpose was to be for dispelling negativity and that it was to be called The Violet Flame. This was the first time that Jeni had heard the name, so was delighted when she discovered more about it.

Both their details are in the Acknowledgements section at the back of the book.

Remember there are no right or wrong ways to use the Violet Flame; you are only limited by your imagination. These are simply suggestions that I have tried and tested.

CHAPTER 4

Summary

Ways to work with the Violet Flame

🔹 There are many different ways to work with the Violet Flame and it is your personal choice as to which methods you use.

🔹 Every action starts with a thought. Combining the power of thought and honest intent with the Violet Flame will ensure the outcome is for the Highest Good.

🔹 Visualisation and meditation are the most popular ways to work with the Violet Flame.

🔹 For those who are not visual, the repetition of Violet Flame decrees, mantras or affirmations will achieve the same effect.

🔹 It also works well to write down those thoughts and intenions that you wish to be transmuted in the Violet Flame.

🔹 You do not have to have any artistic ability to be creative with the Violet Flame. Express your feelings in any way you choose.

🔹 Create a Violet Flame sacred space with related items on a window ledge, table, or any suitable location. Alternatively keep things in a violet coloured box to use whenever you wish.

🔹 Place crystals which resonate with the Violet Flame around your home or work place; create mandalas or wear them as jewellery.

🔹 Violet Flame aura sprays and incense are useful for clearing the energy of any space or room as well as your own personal energy.

🔹 There are no right or wrong ways to use the Violet Flame; it will only work for the Highest Good.

CHAPTER 5

THE VIOLET FLAME - EVERY DAY

Let the Violet Flame become part of your daily routine and work with it to transform your life. If it is done from the heart with pure intent it is for you to choose your own methods to invoke the energy of the Violet Flame. It need never become dull or boring as your imagination can expand with it, constantly finding new ways to focus your intention on creating a more positive life. The more you use it, the stronger it builds, the quicker it forms, and the more effective it can be.

Mountain or molehill?

Problems arise daily, issues that we have to deal with and just the grind of life's routine distracts us from our spiritual journey. At times it is hard to 'rise above' many matters that are of the physical, material world. By drawing on the energy of the Violet Flame every single day, we can deal with these situations more quickly, releasing any negativity before it can take hold and build into a more deep-seated problem.

It takes time to create the most worthwhile changes, and this is no exception. It is not a quick fix; some things may take weeks, some even months to clear, because we are complicated beings and many of our troubles and issues have layers to peel away.

This is a vibrant, constantly moving and changing energy that can make such a huge difference if we continue to use it daily.

If you are caught in a situation that may be affecting you or draining your energy, the Violet Flame is only a thought away!

Quick, daily meditation practices that you can try:

At the beginning of any meditation it is important to follow the grounding routine. This will ensure that you do not feel light-headed at the end of your meditation, whatever your experiences may have been.

"Take three deep breaths in and as you breathe out visualise your roots growing from the soles of your feet. See or feel them entwining around each other, forming into one strong, solid tap-root descending to the core of the Earth". (The full visualisation is in Chapter 3, 'Grounding')

Alternatively, you can repeat three times any phrase that you feel appropriate to ground yourself, for example:

"My roots connect me to the heart of
Mother Earth – I am grounded".

Keeping the 'spark' alight

As a quick daily meditation you can try one of the following:

"Breathe in clear positive Violet Light and breathe out cloudy grey negative light, until you are breathing the Violet Light both in and out. Feel it extending through your entire body to the tips of your fingers and toes, transforming any tiredness, aches and pains, cleansing you of any negativity, doubts, and fears. Breathe it out into your aura until you feel completely violet, peaceful, energised and strong. Imagine a shiny gold layer around the outer edge of your aura to keep your energy protected."

"Bring any regrets, negative feelings, doubts, fears etc to the surface of your body; imagine what they would look like. Watch Violet Flames dance and flicker over your skin or through your aura, burning away each negative emotion in turn, growing bigger and bigger until the Violet Flame surrounds you like a pillar of fire."

Quick re-affirmations

 These can be repeated as often as you like, whenever you feel the need. Take three deep breaths and as you breathe out repeat either of the following to re-ignite the spark:

> "A violet spark lies within my heart,
> The flame is lit, its light expands,
> I am transformed."

or

> "I relight the spark of Violet Flame
> That exists within my heart.
> Its glow spreads through me
> And all around me
> Within my golden shell.
> Cleansed and purified,
> I AM the Violet Flame.

Clear the decks...

Clearing and Protecting Spaces

Frequently places hold negative energy. This needs clearing and once clear it needs protecting to keep it that way. If it is somewhere you regularly spend time, for example your home or work place, then you may prefer to clear it regularly, even daily.

Visualisation:

Stand in the centre of the room you wish to clear and reignite the spark of Violet Flame at your heart centre. Let the glow build and spread throughout your body, breathing in Violet Light and breathing out Violet Light. Push it out into your aura with every out breath, expanding it further and further until it is outside the area you are clearing. Protect the outer limit of Violet Flame energy you have created with a hard, shiny gold shell or golden layer of light.

If you are not physically present you can visualise a spark, star, or tiny pyramid of Violet Flame energy at the centre of the space you wish to clear. Focus your attention on it to give it the energy to grow and expand transmuting all negativity to positive energy as it expands out from the centre. Once the Violet Flame energy has reached beyond the boundary of where you will be, protect the outer layer with a hard shiny gold shell or golden layer of light.

Affirmation:

"I clear this space with Violet Flame
From the centre of the room.
It transmutes all negative energy
To the highest vibration of light."

It's a piece of cake!

Infusing Food, Drink and Water

You can infuse your food and drink with the Violet Flame to transmute any negativity from them. You can do the same to the water you bathe in, as well as the water you give plants and pets and raise their vibrational frequency.

Some suggestions

◆ You can use crystals by placing them in the fridge, fruit bowl or wherever food is stored.

◆ You can place a crystal in a jug of water to infuse it, but just take care the crystal is not transferred to the glass as you pour.

◆ You can write out a mantra and place it on a tray or mat that you use to put food or drink on.

◆ You can set the intent for the Violet Flame to infuse your food and drink through using violet coloured trays or crockery.

◆ You can visualise a stream of Violet Light entering into and clearing through food as you buy it, cook it or eat it.

◆ For your bath or shower you can use crystals or candles around the bathroom or visualise Violet Light within the water.

Rock Chic...

Crystals

If wearing jewellery made with any of the Violet Flame crystals remember to set your intent for it to bring the Violet Flame energy to you every time you put it on. You can do this with your thoughts or by repeating a mantra. There are so many different designs of jewellery; you don't have to weigh yourself down with big chunky stones if that is not your style – a delicate pair of stud earrings carries just the same frequency of energy. Size most certainly does not matter! The same applies to crystals you may carry with you or place in your surroundings.

...to Rock Chick

Music, song and dance

If, like me, you love to have music playing – at home, in the car or anywhere at all – imagine Violet Flames dancing to the music, as if the vibration of sound is fanning the flames. If you fancy yourself as a bit of a singer, (even if strictly alone,) imagine Violet Flames responding to your voice. The energy builds with each increase of volume like a crescendo, then dying down with the quieter, softer tones of your singing. It feels as if the Violet Flame is your audience. Above all, enjoy it!

Traditionally, the music of Strauss is linked to the Violet Flame, as is 'The Rakoczy March' by Franz Liszt. They are said to carry similar sound vibrations and resonate at a very similar frequency. If these are to your taste, all well and good, but if not you can visualise the Violet Flame pulsing even to heavy metal music. I'm a rock chick at heart and like to feel the rhythm pounding through the floor – it brings the Violet Flame up through my feet to pulse with the beat of my heart.

CHAPTER 5

Summary

Incorporating the Violet Flame into your daily life

◆ All sorts of daily situations can soon become problems. Using the Violet Flame every day helps to deal with these as they arise, transmuting any negative thoughts or energy to positivity. The Violet Flame is only a thought away!

◆ The more you use it, the stronger it builds, the quicker it forms, and the more effective it can be.

◆ A quick daily visualisation or repetition of a mantra or affirmation can make all the difference to your day – every day. Make it part of your morning routine, as you get washed, clean your teeth or have your breakfast. You do not need to get up any earlier.

◆ The Violet Flame can be used to clear and protect spaces. Energy builds up wherever people regularly spend time. It helps to clear any negativity from that energy and then keep it clear, in order to feel and work at your best.

◆ Infusing your food and drink with Violet Flame helps you to maintain internal health.

◆ Bathing in the light of violet candles helps relaxation.

◆ Plants and pets love it too! Give them water infused with Violet Flame.

◆ Carry crystals with you or place them around your home to enhance the atmosphere.

◆ Wear jewellery which has crystals of the same vibration as the Violet Flame.

◆ Play any music that you like and imagine Violet Flames moving to the rhythm, sing along with it and visualise the words in violet or dance to your heart's content.

◆ Have fun and enjoy finding ways to focus your energy on the Violet Flame every day, even if only for a few minutes; it will build and strengthen with regular use.

PART TWO

This section of the book shows you how to apply some of the methods I have covered to specific areas of your life. You may like to use this as a reference section, since not all situations will apply at the same time, and not all situations described will exactly fit your own. However I have tried to focus on the main issues of our lives, those that we devote the most time and energy to, and then go into as many different aspects of those as I can. These are all issues that take time to build and progress and so are rarely changed overnight. Do be patient, persevere with the changes you want to bring about, celebrate the slightest progress as that will propel the matter forward and be aware of your expectations; as the saying goes, 'You cannot make a silk purse out of a sow's ear'.

Well, what did you expect?

One of the first steps to applying the Violet Flame to specific areas of your life is to examine your expectations. Your thoughts right from the start will influence the outcome.

Having impossibly high or very fixed expectations will limit the scope of your experience. As an extreme example: by focusing on finding Prince Charming (or Princess Beautiful) to come and take you away to live happily ever after in a castle with servants to wait on you, you may miss a wonderful job that would give you a great deal of satisfaction. You may not get a Prince or Princess, but the person you see at the bus stop every morning might just be your ideal partner. So when you look for change in your life, expect just that and that is what you will get. If you focus on a positive outcome to any change, you will build that positive energy. The Violet Flame will ensure it is for your Highest Good, and that will ensure you learn and grow from an experience that will fulfil your life and your soul's journey.

However, looking at the other side of this coin; if you tend to always focus on the negative side to things you will build that negative energy. If you expect nothing at all, that is what you will get. Your perceptions and negative expectations can really limit the effectiveness of the Violet Flame, so that would be the first thing to transform!

I spoke to a lady who told me, "I keep using the Violet Flame, but nothing's happened, nothing's changed, I'm still in the same situation. So I guess it just doesn't work for me, but nothing ever does."

Her friend pointed out a couple of positive things that had actually changed for her, but they were dismissed by the lady who was feeling so negative.

I asked her what she had expected in the beginning. She replied, "Well, nothing really, I thought I'd give it a try but I think I'll always be on my own and out of work."

I urged her to continue to work with the Violet Flame on her negative perceptions and her low expectations, celebrating even the smallest achievements, however trivial, because that would encourage more change in her life. I do hope she persevered and found the right way for her to incorporate it into her life, creating the changes she so desperately wanted. It has to start from within.

Personal experiences – mine, and those of family members', friends' and clients' – will be included as examples to demonstrate the benefits of working with the Violet Flame. Naturally, for reasons of privacy, I have changed the names of the people whose stories I have featured.

CHAPTER 6

RELATIONSHIPS

This section covers a broad spectrum of relationships and is not confined solely to the romantic. It includes relationships with friends, family, neighbours or work colleagues.

The Violet Flame *can* be used in relationships to attract the right person to you. However, it only works for the Highest Good and cannot be used to bend somebody else's will, to make somebody fall in love with you or change frogs into princes! It is magic, but not that kind!

It can help to create balance and harmony in a relationship by transmuting any difficulties or negative emotions whether at home or in the workplace.

Finally, should any type of relationship end for whatever reason the Violet Flame will help with closure and allow you to move on.

Attract the relationship not the person

By building up the Violet Flame energy in and around you and expanding it out into the world regularly you will attract people who resonate with that energy. So all relationships will then have a stronger foundation for success.

What most people really want to know, however, is how they can attract Miss or Mr Right. It is important to focus on how you would like the relationship to work rather than specific details of a particular person. For example, mutual support and respect, shared interests, same sense of humour rather than 'tall, dark and handsome' or 'a millionaire with a boat'!

You can either write down the sort of relationship you would like and Violet Flame it to attract that type of relationship or could do the following meditation.

Visualisation:

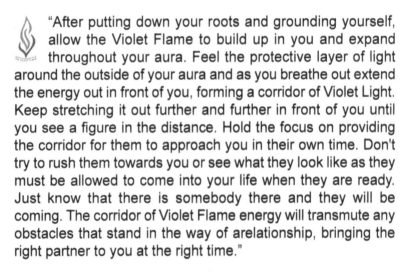 "After putting down your roots and grounding yourself, allow the Violet Flame to build up in you and expand throughout your aura. Feel the protective layer of light around the outside of your aura and as you breathe out extend the energy out in front of you, forming a corridor of Violet Light. Keep stretching it out further and further in front of you until you see a figure in the distance. Hold the focus on providing the corridor for them to approach you in their own time. Don't try to rush them towards you or see what they look like as they must be allowed to come into your life when they are ready. Just know that there is somebody there and they will be coming. The corridor of Violet Flame energy will transmute any obstacles that stand in the way of arelationship, bringing the right partner to you at the right time."

Don't worry if no figure appears; it may not be the right time, so it is worth repeating the visualisation at a later date. You could try the written exercise to help you focus on the type of relationship you are looking for.

Debbie used this visualisation with the intent of attracting her soul mate. At first she saw no one at the end of the corridor but persevered until her soul mate appeared. Being rather impatient, as we all can be, she visualised a man approaching and she went to meet him. She went into 'romantic novel' mode creating a fantasy worthy of Mills and Boon! She was very disappointed that this was not echoed in her real life, and so she asked me what had gone wrong. I reminded her to wait when she saw somebody appear at the end of the corridor and not rush to meet him. We discussed her intent to attract her soul mate and I urged her to focus on the qualities of the relationship she was looking for instead.

A little word here about soul mates. Personally I feel a soul mate is someone you have shared a life with previously. A bond has been created that is still recognised in this lifetime. So meeting a soul mate in this life does not necessarily lead to a romantic relationship. The understanding of these relationships is helped by holding them in the Violet Flame, transmuting any expectations that we still hold. That said, we still naturally yearn for someone we feel such a bond with.

Bearing all this in mind Debbie decided to try again. Several times she practiced just building up the Violet Flame and extending it in to a corridor with no other intent than to provide the opportunity for a relationship to come.

In the course of her work as a florist she met a man who she got on well with. The next time she did the visualisation she was surprised to see he was the one moving towards her along the corridor of Violet Light. She remembered not to rush towards him, but waited patiently. In reality it took him a few weeks to ask her out when he felt a little more sure of his feelings for her. He had many of the qualities that she had looked for and so the relationship flourished.

Build it up, let it grow

Laying the foundations

You can proactively lay the foundations for successful relationships whether at home or work and continue to feed them with positive Violet Flame energy on a regular basis. There are many ways to do this according to your own personal preference and you may try a few different methods before you find one that works for you.

Draw two flame shapes with a violet pen or on violet coloured paper. Write your own name in one flame and the name of the person with whom you are building a relationship in the other. You can link these two flames with a base line, representing the foundation of your relationship. At any time you can add flames to your design to incorporate common goals, for example a business or children. This can be kept on your altar or in your sacred space. Alternatively you could draw or doodle it anywhere at any time and add to it as situations change. If your goals or aims change, burn the drawing in the flame of a violet candle and start again.

Relationships thrive in positive energy. Visualise the Violet Flame surrounding you both, in the place you live or work, creating a bubble of Violet Light. This helps to prevent any outside negativity or interference from affecting your relationship. If this is done regularly, with a daily image or intent, the prospect for happiness and harmony is strengthened.

Round and round and round it goes...
where it stops, nobody knows.

Harmony and equality

The Lemniscate (infinity symbol or basically a figure of eight on its side) can be used to unite or reunite two people, their ideals, their goals and their needs, particularly where some sort of compromise is required. This is a lovely smooth flowing line to draw, going over and over it with your violet pen for example. Write your names, your ideals or goals in each loop; even if they seem quite different the Lemniscate will hold them together and the Violet Flame will flow along the lines as you draw them, connecting them in the centre. You could draw the symbol with just your names in and place it under the bed, to keep the harmony and unity flowing in your sleep and dreams. I know someone who wrote 'Management' in one loop and 'Staff' in the other and stuck it on the underside of the boardroom table where they had their weekly meetings! He said in his mind he re-energised it with Violet Flame before each meeting and swore it worked!

You could imagine the Lemniscate symbol in 3D glowing with Violet Light, looping around you both. This is a powerful symbol and cannot be used to tie someone to you against their will or to hold them to a promise; it is not fixed, but a flowing line of energy allowing you both to retain your individuality whilst connected at the centre which represents the heart of your relationship. The Violet Flame cannot be used for any purpose other than the Highest Good so it would be a waste of time and energy to try to set any other intent.

When my own two children were constantly bickering and arguing as sibling teenagers often do, I drew a Lemniscate, the infinity symbol, with a violet pen and wrote their names in the loops. Every night when I went to bed I imagined the Violet Flame continually running along the line, around them and crossing over in the centre. That centre point eternally connected them, providing a common ground, a point of unity and they gradually achieved a status quo and an acceptance of each other.

This exercise can be used to unite those who are separated by location, different beliefs or understanding, family rifts or any situation which is ongoing.

When the going gets tough...

Dealing with difficulties

Any difficulties or problems within a relationship can be eased by maintaining the energy of the Violet Flame within the home or workplace. Friction anywhere is often best resolved by transmuting the negativity using the exercise in chapter 2 for clearing and protecting spaces.

Isolated incidents can be dealt with quite quickly before negative energy has built up over a period of time. Matters that have been ongoing for longer will naturally take longer to clear. (Changing habits and patterns of behaviour are covered in chapter 8.)

As relationships are so complicated and involved some issues can not be resolved overnight so do keep persevering. Think of it as layers of an onion being peeled off, and deal with each layer or issue one at a time.

Conflict and arguments

As an example of an isolated incident, a couple were arguing loudly and abusively outside my shop. When they started to push and shove each other, I and another member of staff visualised a Violet Light around the pair of them. We called on Kuan Yin to bring her compassion and mercy to their situation and focused the Violet Flame burning off their anger taking the heat out of their argument. It was not long before they moved away, still bickering but no longer violent.

Arguments do arise in the best of relationships and this is totally acceptable as a way to clear the air or express differing views, so not every argument needs to be dissipated.

However if at any time verbal conflict escalates to anger, visualise a wall of Violet Flame to fill the gap between you.

Their anger will then be transmuted through the Violet Flame so that you do not absorb the negative attack. Fighting anger with anger only intensifies the conflict. Creating a barrier of Violet Flame will end it much quicker.

Whether you are witness to or involved in an argument your energy will be affected. You will find as you live in the Violet Flame holding the energy within and around you on a daily basis these types of situations are less likely to occur, and will certainly cease to affect you so badly.

Pump up the volume!

John and Audrey were nearing retirement and lived in a semi-detached property on the outskirts of a big city. They loved their home and the location until new neighbours moved in and it felt as if all hell had broken loose! They were very noisy, played loud music, argued heatedly and had teenage children with friends arriving at all hours on motorbikes. Their worst nightmare became reality and they soon dreaded their retirement, fearing they would have to move or have no peace to enjoy. Not long after the new family moved in, things did quieten down a bit and John and Audrey decided to try to get to know them, hoping that would help the situation as they really wanted to stay and retire there. However the other family saw no reason to keep their noise down and the neighbourly relationship was never going to be harmonious.

I bumped into Audrey soon after this and we went for a coffee. I saw the bags under her eyes as she crumpled into the seat opposite me and said, "I feel as if I haven't slept for weeks!"
She explained what had happened and asked if there was anything, anything at all that I felt could help them. She sounded really desperate! The eldest son had just moved out

with his biker friends so already there was hope. I told her of the Violet Flame and that I had a workshop coming up on how to use it as I felt this was going to be the greatest help to them. We talked through methods of protecting themselves and creating barriers to shield them from the now incessant rowing. The next day both she and John booked onto the workshop. They learnt of the many different ways to use the Violet Flame and came up with one of their own which they have agreed I may share.

At their home, they walked down their adjoining front garden hedge and back fence, and actually carried out a pretend planting of Violet Flames, as if planting candles instead of bulbs. Inside the house they chose and marked places on the skirting board where they would place Violet Flame jets, like gas jets on a cooker, and even marked a place on the adjoining wall for a 'thermostat'. Whenever the family next door had loud music playing for too long or started shouting and swearing at each other, John or Audrey would simply turn up the Violet Flames via the 'thermostat'.

This proved to be another example of people reacting to the energy of the Violet Flame quite subconsciously, without knowing why. Audrey reported that the music would be turned down or off completely and the rows would fizzle out. Although the family are not perfect neighbours and some occasional disruption still continues, John and Audrey feel they have a means of taking control, affecting the amount of upset it had caused them previously.

I was so thrilled that they had followed their own inspirational idea as it was then very personal, and they really enjoyed seeing the effects of their own creation.

Guess what I heard...!

Gossip and misunderstandings

Gossip in the workplace is fairly common, frequently harmless and often best sorted with humour. Similarly, gossip amongst friends can be easily sorted out when the truth comes to light but can also really hurt and cause break ups that were unnecessary. It usually occurs because of lack of communication or misunderstanding. Comments that can become distorted like 'Chinese Whispers' when passed around and embellished each time it's repeated, grow out of all proportion and be very upsetting, causing severe disruption to relationships with colleagues, friends, family or partners.

Jenny worked in a bank and was seen by her colleagues having regular meetings with her manager in his office. A rumour soon went round that she was complaining to him about them and vying for his attention. In actual fact she was working on a confidential project and giving him regular updates. The rumours soon got out of hand and emails about her were sent around the office making her feel isolated and unpopular. As she couldn't tell her colleagues what she was working on she decided to use the Violet Flame to clear the lines of communication. She came into the office early one morning and cleared the office space. She then sat at her desk visualising Violet Flame energy flowing through the wires connecting all computers and telephones. She placed a large Amethyst crystal on her desk anchoring the Violet Flame energy there.

She followed this routine daily linking her workstation with all those of her colleagues maintaining a constant stream of Violet Light between them. Gradually her colleagues came to realise that her meetings with her manager were solely work related and their fears had been unfounded. The Violet Flame had transmuted the negativity that had given rise to the gossip, the misunderstanding cleared even before the project was announced and she was once again accepted by her colleagues.

It's that old Mother-in-Law thing!

Outside influences such as relatives or work

What to do when you just do not get along with your partner's family or friends? I have heard several times that everything is fine in a relationship until other people are involved. One friend of mine point blankly refuses to see or have any contact with her Mother-in-Law, whereas I always felt very lucky with mine and never had any problems. However my ex-husband did have a friend who would turn up like the proverbial bad penny and disrupt our entire household and our relationship, leading to rows after he had left us in shattered pieces again. My ex was very loyal to this friend which in itself I could admire, so I kept that as the positive attribute to focus on, whilst trying to diminish the negative effect he had on us all. It was always a hard battle while he was there as he was a very strong and forceful character, but each time he left I would clear the energy of the house with Violet Flame to transmute all his negative influence. I found over the years that whilst he was staying, it seemed to work best for me to keep myself protected in a bubble of Violet Flame with extra gold around the outside! I tried within my protective energy field to remain calm and unaffected by his presence, but the minute he was gone I felt a huge sigh of relief as the Violet Flame cleansed and restored the atmosphere in our home. All my Violet Flame crystals were cleansed too as I thanked them for transmuting the negative energy and I got through more aura sprays then, than at any other time!

Although I continued to find this one friend very difficult I did once receive a lovely 'thank you' card from him saying that he knew it was not easy for me to have him there as he had always been a bad influence on my husband, but that whenever he visited us he felt somehow more determined to make things right in his own life. I have no ending to this episode as I had no further contact with him when my husband and I parted company, but sometimes I wonder...

Creating balance and harmony in relationships is not just about resolving conflicts and misunderstandings; sometimes it is more about maintaining the common ground, keeping the lines of communication open and the flow of energy between you. Occasionally it is also about letting go and moving on.

> ### *"To be or not to be?"*
> – William Shakespeare *Hamlet*

Natural endings and maintaining links

Sometimes friendships and relationships do naturally come to an end, circumstances change and people move on. These endings are usually smoother but often are the ones that have no closure because we like to keep them open in case our paths cross again. Maintaining a thread of Violet Flame energy between you keeps that opportunity alive, with no regrets for the time that has lapsed, allowing you to renew that friendship or relationship again in the future should you so wish.

Many years ago I had to move away from the area I lived and leave behind a very dear friend. We had shared a lot over several years and it was a hard wrench to move. At the time I knew nothing consciously of the Violet Flame, but have many times since sent it back to that time and I constantly maintain it as a link to her and her family. We are still in regular contact and the bond of friendship between us is still strong despite the distance in miles. The Violet Flame bridges any gap of Time or Space.

That's it! I've had enough!

Finding the courage to end it

Even when lessons have been learnt and it's time to move on there are many cases when we still hang on to relationships that are long past their 'sell by' date. There are many reasons for this; fear of being alone, fear of causing or being hurt or even fear of change. For whatever reason, the longer we continue the more difficult it becomes to end it. Fear can be transmuted by the Violet Flame, giving us the courage to end a relationship that is no longer for our highest good. Even when this comes as a great relief it is still worth focusing on the Violet Flame to allay any feelings of guilt that may ensue.

> Dave came to see me, rather sheepishly, because he could not find the courage to leave his domineering wife. Even though he had made his decision many months previously, fed up with her verbal and emotional battering, his self-esteem was so low that he doubted he could ever get out of the situation he was in. He was a quiet, gentle and spiritual man only in his thirties, who had chosen a wife who would take control and run the home and family leaving him in peace to pursue his hobby of woodturning and carving. He said he was now spending long hours in his workshop to stay away from her and she continually put him down in front of their friends and family. The situation was made so much more difficult as they had a little girl of about three years old whom Dave felt he couldn't abandon. I pointed out that there were many issues here that needed professional input, counselling, family mediation and solicitors but that I could help him find the courage to take the first step. That was all he wanted, he said. He was well aware of the path he would have to follow but felt unable to even start.
>
> As he had already shown courage in coming to me and admitting his situation, I felt that was a good starting point.

He said he was quite visual, that he could imagine what he could carve from a piece of wood before he started and would like to try a meditation. I talked him through the grounding routine of sending a root down to the centre of the Earth to the iron core, with smaller roots spreading out to connect to the roots of trees and the wood element that he so loved to work with.

When he was fully relaxed, I asked him, "Think of the spark of courage that brought you here today; where is it located within your physical body?" (The most common place is within the solar plexus or the Hara centre but could be anywhere.) He said that it was hidden in his side, under his ribs.

"What does it look like?" A box, he told me. "Imagine its colour, size and shape. Start to feel it as an actual item inside you. Acknowledge your courage as something real and tangible, just like the heart that was given to the lion in the 'Wizard of Oz'. It was not a physical heart but a representation of courage for him, just as your box is for you."

I then suggested that he opened the lid of the box. "Is there anything inside it?" He said that it was empty.

I had told him of the Violet Flame and he had already experienced the spark of it at his heart. I told him to imagine expanding the Flame, feeding it with his breath, sending beams of light like lasers to the area where his courage was hiding behind his ribs. I said, "Every time you breathe out, fill the box with Violet Light until it is full and then close the lid. Expand the Violet Light throughout your entire body and aura transmuting any other negative thoughts and doubts."

"Return your focus to where your box of Violet Flame is and know that the box is your courage. It is within you and you may take it out, enlarge it or release the Violet Flame from it whenever you need to."

"Do you wish it to stay hidden beneath your ribs?" I asked him. He said he would move it to just below his heart so that he could feel it there ready, and that when he opened the lid, the Violet Flame would illuminate his heart and his throat chakra so that he would have the courage to say what he needed to say.

He found his courage, moved out of the family home and managed to sort out all the practicalities.

Now I feel really guilty!

To allay feelings of guilt

 To allay any feelings of guilt when ending a relationship you can carry or wear a piece of amethyst or sugilite crystal and repeat a decree or mantra such as:

"I live my life in the Violet Flame
       - Releasing all my guilt and shame"

Sugilite's healing properties are probably the best when working with this issue, so try placing one under your pillow at night, or creating a mandala over your own name to help release any guilt. Forgiveness is extremely important; remember to forgive yourself!

If you enjoy meditation or visualisation then imagine the flame at your heart pushing all the guilt out from your centre and 'burning it off' in Violet Flames that flicker over your skin until your aura is clear and light.

It's not you... it's me

Anger and bewilderment

When the other party ends the relationship and we feel hurt, betrayed, angry, or bewildered we tend to blame ourselves even when we are reassured that it is not our fault. These feelings can be transmuted in the Violet Flame by writing them down and burning them in the flame of a violet candle. As you watch the flame burning away your written words feel the Violet Flame burning away the hurt and anger. Repeat this as often as you like until the negative feelings have gone.

Your new mantra or affirmation could be:

 "Within the Violet Flame I am free"

It's a black hole

Loss and emptiness

The sense of loss when a partner decides to leave suddenly without warning has been likened to a 'black hole' in space. The feelings of grief are similar to a sudden bereavement and yet often there is still some contact even if it is only the collection of belongings or practical arrangements. This is a situation that is hard to close and accept as we tend to be ever hopeful of a reunion. So the 'black hole' sucks in the relationship and that disappears, but it leaves us on the edge looking at nothing whilst we search for clues as to a reason for the ending.

A friend of mine, Mary, who also works a lot with the Violet Flame, helped her neighbour through this situation by offering him a round piece of black card to represent his 'black hole', and a pin. She asked him to stab the centre of the black card with the pin every time a word came into his mind which described how he felt. 'Despair' went into the middle and pierced the card, so did 'Why?' and 'Empty' followed by several others – not all repeatable here! Mary held the card up to the light and he saw all the pin pricks letting the light through. Then she stuck some violet coloured acetate film to the back of the card so that he could see violet coloured light coming through. She taught him how to utilise the Violet Flame to let all his sense of loss and emptiness pass through the holes into the Violet Light he could see behind the blackness.

I thought this was most innovative of her and she said it certainly seemed to help him as a start to piercing the blackness he felt. She showed him other ways too but this she said was the 'spark' that set the ball rolling to gradual and eventual acceptance and recovery.

Making peace with the past

Closure, moving on and letting it go

The Violet Flame can give closure after a relationship has ended whether it is at the time or even at a much later date.

Sarah had her heart broken by Robert, a man she felt was her soul mate. The relationship ended suddenly when without warning he left her for another woman. There was no closure, just anger, bitterness and pain. For many years she found it very difficult to speak to other men and became cynical and mistrusting. Gradually she learnt to accept that not all men are the same and could have male friends again. But the bitterness towards Robert remained. When she came to learn about the Violet Flame and its balancing effect on past issues, she kept going through the exercise to take the Violet Flame back to the time when their relationship ended so badly.

She visualised the time and place of their last meeting, seeing him with the other woman. She brought it into really sharp focus by recalling as many details as she could: colours, smells, sounds, expressions. She visualised, over and over again, the re-enactment of the final confrontation taking place within the glow of the Violet Flame.

Each time it seemed less of a shock as she gradually came to accept the break up and was able to visualise it without the emotional upset it had caused her for so many years. In time and with her spiritual awareness growing, her perceptions of it changed and she came to understand that he had merely fulfilled his part in her life's experiences, that we all learn the most through the hardest lessons. Working regularly with the Violet Flame on herself, she was able to understand and forgive him. Eventually she felt able to thank him for creating the situation that had enabled her to feel the absolute physical, mental and emotional pain of a broken heart, realising that it would have been something she had chosen to experience this lifetime, and as connected souls he would have volunteered to be the 'bad guy' out of love.

Sarah continued to visualise him surrounded by Violet Light, both at the time of the break up and through his life since. Within the light of the Violet Flame she imagined his face beginning to smile and that image in her mind would make her smile too. It did not take him long to pick up on the energy she was sending out.

Thirteen years after she had last seen him, he got in touch with her and they arranged to meet. He had since married and had children, but he still carried some guilt from knowing he had hurt Sarah all those years ago. He had decided that it was time to say he was sorry. Sarah felt sure that this sudden contact after all the years could only be due to the Violet Flame.

At their meeting, they were able to talk through their past relationship. She explained how her hurt and bitterness had finally gone as her spiritual understanding of karma had grown. He was relieved to find she was able to forgive him and admitted to having been very nervous on his way to their meeting. He could now let go of his guilt and regret, leaving no outstanding issues between them. Towards the end of their meeting Robert commented that the room was filled with mauve light, so Sarah then told him that she had been working with the Violet Flame. He had never heard of it!

They have kept in touch occasionally and remain friends.

CHAPTER 6

Summary

Relationships

♦ Attract the relationship not the person. Focus on the qualities of the relationship that you want and the Violet Flame will ensure the outcome is positive.

♦ Meeting a soul mate in this life does not necessarily lead to a romantic relationship but the Violet Flame can help you to under stand all these relationships.

♦ Working with the Violet Flame will help the positive growth of any relationship, not just the romantic kind.

♦ Isolated problems can be dealt with quite quickly with the Violet Flame. Matters that have been ongoing for longer will naturally take longer to clear.

♦ Use the Violet Flame as a way of protecting you and your home from other's negativity or outside influences.

♦ When relationships come to an end, the Violet Flame can assist closure or can transform and maintain a connection, if appropriate.

♦ The Violet Flame can give us the courage to end a relation ship that is no longer for our Highest Good.

♦ Guilt, anger and bewilderment can all be transmuted by the Violet Flame so that relationship endings can be less painful for all concerned.

♦ The Violet Flame can ease the sense of loss when a relationship ends suddenly.

◆ We learn the most from the hardest lessons. Our lessons can
be understood and completed more easily with the mercy
and forgiveness of the Violet Flame.

CHAPTER 7

JOB AND CAREER MATTERS

Whether you are self-employed, employed or unemployed, job and career matters can take up a large proportion of your time and energy. Most people spend much of their lives 'at work' and nobody on their death bed mutters 'I wish I'd spent more time at the office!' The aim of using the Violet Flame in relation to your job or career is to make your working life productive and happy.

Confucius said that if you enjoy your job you will never have to work. It certainly is true that doing what you love does not seem like hard work, so by using the Violet Flame to find the job or career that suits you best, you can avoid feeling like 'a square peg in a round hole' or weighed down with a job you hate. However I would point out that if you have two left feet no amount of 'Violet Flaming' will turn you in to a premiership footballer! It is not about aiming for the best paid job or fame; it is about finding what best suits your individual skills and needs.

It is quite unusual for situations at work to remain the same throughout your entire career. The Violet Flame can help with those changes, any differences or disputes that may arise, maintaining the balance and harmony with work colleagues, bosses and anybody associated with your business. When a job or your career ends the Violet Flame can help you to adjust to those changes too.

Self employed - be your own boss

Finding the right work for you

Finding the right job or line of work for you can be very time-consuming and take a lot of energy, particularly if you have a variety of options. No one can tell you what job you should be doing, although sometimes it helps to take an honest look at your skills, talents and interests whatever they may be and however trivial or simple they may seem. Try making a list of these using a violet coloured pen or paper and use the Violet Flame to see what words or images come to mind linking the words on your list.

Susan was always artistic and found it very hard to focus on commonly advertised jobs; nothing ever seemed to quite fit so she wrote down a list of things she liked doing, the way she liked to work and what she wanted from a job. Her list included:

Art/Painting
Creative imagination
Science fiction/Fantasy books and films
Sewing
Design
Fine detailed work
Fun
Working from home in own time
One off, individual creations
Travel and exploring, meeting new people

Susan visualised her list surrounded by Violet Light and held the Violet Flame within her, opening her heart and mind to any potential or possibilities that may arise. Within the light some words seemed to be illuminated, shining brightly. Her eyes kept being drawn to the same words as if they were jumping up from the page, creating an image in her mind.

The illuminated words 'painting' and 'fine detailed work' brought to her mind an image of a dolls' house with tiny hand painted ornaments and china sets. She quickly made a note and refocused her attention on her list to see what else would come. With the words 'sewing', 'fine detailed work' and 'one off, individual creations' she saw a beautiful, beaded wedding dress. Finally with the words 'sewing', 'fun', 'science fiction' and 'creative imagination' she saw people in a parade wearing alien fancy dress costumes. With these three ideas forming a new list she focused the Violet Flame energy on each in turn. It was not long before she found a shop in London that outsourced dolls house accessories for private collectors. She visited the shop and found they had been looking for somebody else to design and paint china tea and dinner services. After submitting a sample of her work they were happy to give her commissions that she could do in her own time at home.

Over many years she was asked to make wedding dresses, first through family and friends and as her reputation grew so did her portfolio. The fun side of sewing for her was making fancy dress costumes which she did mainly for charities, carnivals and children's parties. Later she also trained and worked very successfully as a restorer and painter of old clock dials which led to her travelling and meeting people from the world of antiques. So her intent from working with the Violet Flame on her career carried forward through time to fulfil her wishes on many levels.

Sometime later in her life it was pointed out by a good friend that she had not actually included on her list or asked for, any financial reward. This had never occurred to her as money was not an important issue to her. However, she had always struggled with an irregular income, never being able to plan or budget. She revised her list and asked for the ability to earn enough to cover her needs, using the Violet Flame to bring about a more stable future.

Although the Violet Flame cannot be used for gaining riches, as part of a whole career path it is acceptable to ask for your needs to be met.

Promoting yourself

Attracting customers or clients

If you are self-employed and wish to promote your business or service you can use the Violet Flame to accompany your adverts, flyers, business cards and website. There are a number of methods you could apply. Feel yourself filled with Violet Flame energy whilst you are working on your advertising or website and it will spread throughout. If appropriate try incorporating the colour in your design, or simply place your advertising material on your altar.

To set your intent through visualisation, imagine all your flyers, business cards or emails with a ribbon of Violet Light attached spreading out to all who may buy your products or use your service. Hold the other end of the ribbon, so that all potential clients and customers will be able to find you with ease. This will attract to you those who will have the most advantageous effect on your business. As word of mouth recommendations are always the best advertising, these clients and customers who have been attracted to you through the Violet Flame will be the ones to help your business grow.

You can use violet coloured files and folders to hold your records, diaries and business papers and regularly infuse them with Violet Flame energy. Do not write your accounts in violet though as it does not photocopy well and really annoys the accountants!

Prepare for success

In setting up your own business, you are required to take on many different roles: Managing Director, Advertising Executive, Goods and Supplies Buyer, Customer Services Operative, Repair Engineer, Secretary, Personnel Officer (even if you only have one member of staff), and even Tea Maker. Do not be daunted by all these roles and requirements, it can be a lot of fun to be your own boss. Just holding the Violet Flame within you on a daily basis will help you to transform from one role to another with the greatest ease. Focus the Violet Flame on the positive outcome of any task that you undertake and keep referring to your long term plan, seeing that surrounded by Violet Light to prepare for success.

'Amethyst'

After several years of being self employed, working from home on a small scale, I decided with a friend to set up a spiritual shop combined with a healing and teaching centre in Bournemouth. Together we drew up our plans of exactly what we wanted to achieve, the type of property that would suit our purpose, the rent we wanted to pay, the look and feel of the shop and the stock we wanted, the rooms for healing and the space for teaching. Then we infused the plans with Violet Flame to remove any negativity, anything that would stand in the way of achieving those plans and placed a piece of amethyst over the top of them. We chose to call the centre 'Amethyst' as we had both worked with the Violet Flame and it was my passion even then. Daily we would invoke all the help of the Guardians and Masters of the Violet Flame, and searched the internet for a commercial property to rent at the amount we had specified in our business plan. It took just one week.

We both felt that it was for the Highest Good that we create such a centre in that location and so set the intent, had the will to make it happen and then trusted the Violet Flame to do the rest. We similarly found just the right financial support, suppliers, builders to renovate the property and equipment we needed. From viewing the empty shop to opening day was just three months – exactly what we had allowed for, at the cost we had specified (well, a little over budget!) and 'Amethyst' opened in March 2007.

> *"Oh bother!" said Pooh to Piglet*
> – A. A. Milne

Facing difficulties early on

Sometimes situations occur early on in your business that make you doubt whether you have done the right thing in becoming self-employed. Additional legalities, licences, business rates, insurances and the like often come as a nasty surprise shortly after you start. Any difficulties or doubts about being self employed can be transmuted in the Violet Flame allowing you to create a positive outcome. Overcoming these early on will give you the confidence to tackle any future situations with ease.

Even with the smooth set up of Amethyst we had a few difficulties that we used the Violet Flame to resolve. The most memorable of these was the obstinacy of our landlord over a built-in cupboard in the shop with a sink and water heater which had been used as mini kitchen facility. We wanted to remove it as it was unsightly and in a prominent position but the landlord wanted it to remain. Although not in itself enough to make us doubt our decision to open the shop, it was an annoying setback to our plans.

We took a photograph of the open cupboard and put it in our transparent purple document file, building up the Violet Flame within ourselves, expanding it in to the file so that it seeped into the photograph. We started to sense alternative potential uses and images, visualising it as an empty cupboard with the doors removed, and ideas flooded in to fill the space.

Eventually we disconnected the heater, boarded over the sink and hid the taps, ensuring it could be returned to its original state. We filled it with branches, moss and leaves. We strung fairy lights through the branches, painted a moon on the dark back wall, laid an irregular shaped mirror tile on the floor to represent a lake and filled the cupboard with fairies! It became a feature of the shop and people would come in particularly to see our fairy grotto, never guessing what it had once been.

Following on from this we knew that any future disagreements with our landlord could be resolved within the Violet Flame. However, other problems such as disputing an invoice, delivery of goods, quality control issues, dealings with the tax man and so on cropped up from time to time, all of which we dealt with using the Violet Flame to help. Disputes over the phone were always assisted by visualising the Violet Flame flowing through the wires to reach the person at the other end, even tying a violet coloured ribbon to the receiver and at the connection point in the wall socket to hold our intent! Letters and files were always kept in violet folders and any records of difficult situations stored on the computer had the font changed to something attractive in violet and kept in a separate folder so their energy did not affect any other stored correspondence until it was resolved.

Expectations – How difficult can it be?!

Whether you are self-employed or in employment and you ask someone to do a task, you quite rightly expect it to be done, especially if you are paying someone else to do it. Unnecessary stress and frustration is felt when this expectation is not met; the task is not done to the specifications or worse still, not done at all. Personally I find this with advertising, sending in copy and details of colour, font and layout which are then changed or ignored. This creates far more work than is necessary. When it is returned to me as a proof to be sanctioned I check that the original instructions were clear and then confirm that the copy I have sent is the one I want to be used. I visualise a sphere of Violet Flame energy dropping like a water bomb within their energy field. This will transmute the negativity and frustration clearing the way for a positive solution. I find using Violet Flame spheres much more instant and magic and somehow very satisfying!

When the dust settles, the wind blows

Adjusting to changes

When personal circumstances changed and I had to continue running the business on my own, it was daunting at first. Living and working in the light of the Violet Flame certainly helped me to transmute any doubts I had. I found that 'time' was the most difficult element to control. I knew that being self employed and running my own business would involve long hours, but had no idea quite how long! I soon got into the habit of writing my daily tasks in a violet coloured notebook, and repeated a daily mantra that all these jobs would be easily achieved when done within the Violet Flame. I asked for the help of Lady Portia, St. Germain's twin flame, to bring balance and justice to all that I had to do. I never finished the list before more tasks were added but at least the energy flowed continuously without grinding me to a halt.

Sadly, due to the recession at the time, 'Amethyst' had to close after three years and I again faced the huge transition back to working on my own. I am still tremendously grateful for the experience, and was able to move on with only disappointment, but no bitterness or regrets. The Violet Flame still connects the staff, and many of the regular customers and clients from there.

Emma, who has helped me so greatly with the writing of this book, came to 'Amethyst', learnt of the Violet Flame, and a bond of friendship grew from it. She has adapted to great changes in her life since with an ease that has astounded many of her friends and family, rising to challenges with inspirational strength. Having been a high-powered executive, she has also experienced teaching English in South America as a volunteer. By following her heart and making changes to her life with the use of the Violet Flame, she has adapted to these vastly different environments!

When a storm rages

Dealing with major disputes

Whether you are the boss of a company or a one man band, the buck stops with you. The ultimate responsibility for dealing with difficulties or disputes is yours. It may be a dispute with or amongst staff, with suppliers, landlord or local council.

Marion and Fred had taken early retirement to fulfil their dream of running an old-fashioned tea shop. Having ploughed their savings into the business, they built it up to be a popular addition to the Cornish town they had moved to. All seemed to be going well until one morning they found the basement was flooded. All their stocks and supplies were ruined. A dispute ensued between the landlord, the insurance company and the local council when it was found that the flooding had occurred due to cracked drains in the communal alley between their tea shop and the property next door. Marion and Fred's own insurance covered the stock but the long term responsibility and repair of the drains was still outstanding weeks later when I heard of their predicament from a mutual friend. I heard the situation was beginning to really get them down as the smell of damp was pervading their tea shop and discouraging their customers.

I sent a message back to them to first of all visualise a spark of Violet Flame at the centre of their tea shop growing in to a flame with its glow expanding throughout the building including the basement. I asked them to feel the same energy surrounding each of them with a protective layer of gold light around the shell of their auras. If they could daily maintain this image and intent it would protect them from the negative dispute over whose ultimate responsibility the problem was.

In order to manifest the desired outcome to this I suggested they write down on a violet piece of paper a successful resolution to the dispute, describing their business restored with repairs to the drains completed and all trace of dampness gone. They placed this in their favourite ornamental teapot in their window display and used it as a daily focus for their intent that the Violet Flame transmutes any obstacles in the way of success. I also posted them four amethyst tumble stones to place one in each corner of the basement. They later told me they had bought a charoite stone to add to the teapot – an excellent choice as it combats others' negativity. Whilst the dispute continued between the council and the landlord, he did bring them some dehumidifiers to ease the problem until it was finally resolved. Marion and Fred used the Violet Flame again to clear the energy of the basement and the teashop and rewrote their manifestation of increased business to keep in the teapot.

In employment - have your work cut out for you

Applying for a job

It can be fantastic when all goes smoothly and you get the first job you apply for, but any rejections can be quite soul destroying, lowering self confidence and having a negative effect on motivation, often leading to apathy. These frustrations can be transmuted within the Violet Flame to bring about a positive outcome.

If you find a job advertised that you feel would suit your skills, talents and job requirements you can use the Violet Flame to ensure your application is received and looked at in a favourable light. If the application is in paper format you can hold the letter or form you are sending in your hands, feel the spark of Violet Flame at your heart, expand the energy throughout you, feel it flowing through your hands and into the letter or form until it is infused with the energy.

Alternatively if the application is online you could write down the following statement on a piece of violet paper and stick it on to one corner of your computer screen, afterwards placing it on your altar with an amethyst crystal.

"My application for this job
carries the Violet Flame energy to........."
(Insert name of person or organisation to whoever it is being sent.)

This is a very good situation to meditate on; visualise watching yourself as if in a film, walking in to the place of your intended employment and see a pulsating Violet Light all around you. See yourself asking for the right department or whoever you are supposed to meet for an interview and follow the process through to being offered the job, all the while extending the Violet Flame energy to all those you come into contact with. Bring your energy back to the present and continue to visualise the Violet Flame energy within the place you wish to work.

Repeat this meditation as often as you can; add in more details each time to build the energy and strengthen the intent. If you can physically go to the place or building, you can then use the details you have actually seen to make it more realistic.

Do not be despondent if you do not get the first job you apply this method to. Other factors have to be taken into consideration such as other applicants, ultimate suitability and whether it is actually the right job for you in the long term. Rejections can be very demoralising so do focus on a list of your skills, talents and qualifications, adding in things like hobbies and other interests to widen the field of potential. You might like to include in your meditation asking St Germain for help in this matter. He is one of the Directors of the Violet Flame and could redirect your intent to somewhere that is more appropriate for you that you may not have previously considered. Be open to other possibilities or opportunities that arise and remember to thank St Germain if they do.

Maintaining the Violet Flame within yourself daily will help you to remain positive as it transforms any negative thoughts, doubts and fears that tend to surface during the process of job hunting. Remember, as part of your daily routine, to feel the spark of Violet Flame at your heart chakra bursting into flame and the glow spreading through you to fill your entire body and aura.

Go for it!

Attending interviews

Along with the usual preparations for an interview, strengthen the Violet Flame within you.

 Just before you enter the interview room, as you take a deep breath, feel you are breathing out Violet Light into the room, filling it completely. You will be in a room full of positive energy to bring about the right outcome for all concerned. As you leave the room set the intent that all the Violet Flame energy you have built up is absorbed into your job application and any notes that were taken by the interviewer. Hold yourself within Violet Flame energy in the days that follow whilst you are waiting to hear the outcome.

Other methods you might like to try in advance of the interview are:

Write your name and the job title on a piece of paper (in violet if you like), hold the paper and extend the Violet Flame into it. Keep it with you during the interview in your pocket or handbag and when you get home place it on your altar.

Carry a Violet Flame crystal with you or wear a piece of jewellery containing one. Crystals that carry the Violet Flame energy are listed in Chapter 3. Infuse the crystal or piece of jewellery with your intent for a successful outcome. Then, when you are in the interview, you can concentrate on the questions being asked without undue anxiety.

Got it!

Once you have been accepted into employment it is a wonderful opportunity to take the Violet Flame into a new environment. If you work at a desk or counter, you may like to keep a crystal such as amethyst there; it is a very commonly known one that people generally accept. If you can stand at the approximate centre of the basement or ground floor of the building you work in, you can anchor a Violet Flame there, its influence will spread up through the entire building and people will respond to the change in energy even without knowing why.

When I closed 'Amethyst', I rented a treatment room in a building that had an advertising and media firm upstairs. I anchored the Violet Flame in my room, and was told by the staff and the boss of the firm that they liked me being there because the energy seemed to have changed since I took on the room; they were busier than ever, and working in a happy atmosphere. The boss was open minded so I told him what I do; he looked rather bemused, but referred to it several times afterwards.

Alternatively you may like to visualise setting small Violet Flame jets within the walls just as John and Audrey did between them and their neighbours. If you have a computer to work on, choose a screen saver that reminds you of the Violet Flame; other people will respond to its energy. You could even just keep the colour around you, wearing it or crystal jewellery as a reminder that you carry the energy of transformation within you. Anything is possible and the more you do, the stronger it grows.

"Stress - the storm before the calm"
– Author unknown

Work-related stress

Stress at work is one of the most common causes of illness. Time taken off work is frequently blamed on stress; at worst it may even lead to a heart attack, at best it weakens our immune system and our ability to cope. So it is important to have some way of tackling stress so that it does not build up into an insurmountable problem. This is frequently a daily occurrence so finding a way of coping with stress that you can utilise at work is important. Aura sprays do help, so does repeating a silent mantra or affirmation, holding a Violet Flame crystal or breathing your feelings into it to be transmuted. Visualisations of the Violet Flame also help when you can grab a moment to yourself and take a few deep breaths holding your focus on transmuting the stress, worry or frustration.

Not many people arrive home after a busy day at work to say that it was fine, no problems arose and work was enjoyable. Most arrive home with some degree of anger or frustration over things that had not gone smoothly. There are many ways to utilise the Violet Flame to negate the feelings before arriving home, such as:

◆ Imagine your car or transport home filled with Violet Light with the intent that all negativity will be transmuted on the journey.

◆ Drive through an imaginary 'car wash' of Violet Flame energy to wash off the day before you get home.

◆ You can use an aura spray to clear your energy and your work-station before you leave. This also ensures you come back to a clear space the next morning.

◆ Repeat a Violet Flame affirmation or mantra on your way home, and perhaps make an effort to not take work home.

Anger and Frustration

I am reminded of a lady I met who told me this was a real problem for her, that she would arrive home from a stressful day in an office of a large corporation and would then unload it all on her poor husband, sometimes moaning for nearly an hour about work while they cooked and ate their dinner.

Alison suspected that he no longer listened as she told him of all the troubles at her work. When she found out from someone else that Steve was also under a huge amount of pressure in his job with threatened closures, she felt guilty that her anger had stopped him from sharing his concerns with her. She promised to change.

Alison and Steve sat down and talked, realising that it was not only the stress at work that was causing the problem but the anger she brought home was spreading to him, into the food they cooked and ate, ruining their dinner time. Because time was precious when they got home from work, Alison chose just to write briefly in violet the name of whoever had caused a problem or sparked her anger, or just a couple of words as an indicator of a situation and then screwed the piece of paper up into a tight ball. She found this quite satisfying and said she would often let out an "Aaaaarggghhh!!!" as she did it! She held the ball of paper up to her mouth and took in a deep breath, feeling the Violet Flame build up within her which she then blew forcefully into the ball of paper. Sometimes she felt it took two or three blows before she could just throw the ball of paper into the bin, and get on with dinner. She did this every night on arriving home, even on the odd days when she had nothing to write except the "Aaaaarrggghhh!!!"

Alison started to use the same method at work, without writing anyone's name or any situation. She called it: 'Blowing away her silent scream'. As her anger and frustration diminished she coped better at work, gradually becoming less tetchy and aggressive herself, feeling more relaxed and popular amongst her co-workers. She was also able to be more supportive of Steve and their dinner times became sacred where nothing negative was to be mentioned! She could not believe that something so simple had made such a vast difference to their lives.

"Nature provides exceptions to every rule
- Why shouldn't we?"

– Author unknown

Rules and regulations

Changes inflicted on the workforce by those in authority can seem at best petty and unnecessary, at worst disruptive and costly.

Tom had direct experience of this whilst working at a well known chain store. It had long been a perk of the job that anything broken, no longer saleable or usable could be taken by any member of staff with a signed permission slip from their department manager. A new store manager decided that this created potential for misuse and loss of revenue. A directive was issued to all departments that in future anything taken out of the store for any reason required a lengthy form filled in with details of retail value, whether it had been used or not, its scrap value (if any), and signed by a department manager and a member of senior management. Any goods that had previously been stock as opposed to display material would then be available to purchase at a percentage of the retail value even if it was broken and destined for the skip. This upset many members of staff who felt they were not trusted by the new store manager. Tom felt particularly aggrieved as he had previously been allowed to take home packaging and ex-display items which he gave to his wife Stephanie who ran an art and craft group at a local community centre. He complained bitterly on finding out that he still had to fill in a form to have even these items of no commercial value. 'Rules were rules and must apply to everybody' he was told. So he told Stephanie that he could not longer help her out in this way.

Stephanie just smiled and said:
"Leave it to me"!

She took her camera in to her next art and craft session and photographed the people there creating items from the waste material that Tom had given her. When she printed off the photographs she infused them with Violet Flame setting the intent that when the store manager saw them he would reinstate the previous system for removal of these items of no monetary value. She made an appointment to see the new store manager and for the week before the meeting she focused this intent daily on the photographs which she had put in a violet coloured envelope to contain the energy of the Violet Flame.

She visualised the meeting surrounded in Violet Light so that when she arrived she felt confident that he would agree to her request. The outcome was that he would not make any concessions regarding Tom taking this material home. However he was happy to make arrangements for such items to be set aside if she was willing to collect them weekly. Colleagues from other departments soon heard of this arrangement and joined in on the scheme and she ended up with more craft material than before.

Tom told her some months later that the store manager had reported this scheme back to head office citing it as one of his achievements in this store. The scheme had been adopted throughout the chain as a way of meeting targets of recycling!

That's not fair!

Uneven distribution of workload

 It does cause a lot of upset if one person is carrying the workload of another through laziness or incompetence. In this situation the Violet Flame can help to restore the balance. Should this be the case for you, try writing your name in large letters and the name of the person you are carrying in small letters. Repeating your names down the page, write yours smaller and smaller and theirs larger until they are of equal size. Tear off the list above where the names are equal and burn it in the flames of a violet candle. Keep the piece of paper with your names written equally and place it on your altar.

Alternatively you could repeat the following positive affirmation:

"I invoke the Violet Flame to restore the balance of workload between (insert your name) and (insert name of other person) ensuring it is just and fair."

Unrealistic demands

If redundancies have cut staff to levels where the smaller work-force has to cover the jobs of those who have left, it can leave individuals feeling overwhelmed and exhausted. The Violet Flame can work for them on a personal level boosting their own energy levels and immune system so that they can cope with the increased demand.

To boost your own energy levels, regularly maintain the Violet Flame within you and protect the outer edge of your aura with a layer of golden light. Try doing this before and after work for a sustained period of time; you'll find it gets quicker with practice and becomes automatic.

If part of your day is spent on trivial jobs that distract you from the main core of your work with no one to delegate them to, make a list of those jobs and draw Violet Flames over the top of them. Visualise yourself doing those tasks surrounded in a Violet Light so that they are accomplished more easily and smoothly.

Lesley was a Community Nurse attached to a day unit for people with mental health problems. Staff levels at the unit were cut drastically from a total of twenty-two down to just nine. As one of the nine left, Lesley, a senior member of staff with many years of psychiatric nursing experience, had to undertake the time-consuming administration jobs such as banking, dealing with emails and correspondence and collecting supplies instead of spending her time with patients and providing the support that they needed.

In her frustration she asked me how the Violet Flame could help her situation. I suggested that she write a list of how ideally she would spend her working day such as: Visiting patients, arranging their support and care packages, consulting with their doctors, etc. She then chose some crystals that carry the Violet Flame energy and placed them in a pattern around her list creating a mandala to focus energy on the primary aspects of her work.

Her choices:
Ametrine, the combination of Amethyst and Citrine which assists with achieving goals, Sugilite, for forgiveness and for seeing the potential results with hope and optimism, and a piece of Hematite at the centre, which although not linked to the Violet Flame is very grounding to anchor the energy of the other stones.

I also gave her a Charoite pendant to wear which protects against any negative thoughts and emotions of others as the disgruntled complaints from the remaining team were getting her down.

Even though the situation could not be changed, her perceptions did. She began to see the core of her job, like the Hematite at the centre of her mandala, as the core of her focus, with the administrative tasks fitting in around it.

She integrated the new tasks into her daily routine of patient visits, she hardly noticed the time spent doing them and no longer felt she was neglecting her patients.

On the move...

Changes, whether they are instigated by yourself or others, can be particularly hard to deal with when they are work-related. For many people work or career defines them and gives them their sense of self worth. It is what people ask when they meet you for the first time:

"What do you do?" so naturally it is an important part of who we are. When our role changes, for any reason, we have to redefine ourselves and this takes quite a big adjustment. As the Violet Flame is transformational energy, it is only fitting that we use this energy to transform our concept of who we are, what we do and how others see us.

Moving up...

Promotion

 Changing other's perceptions of your capabilities can be a stumbling block when moving up in your career. One of the easiest ways to use the Violet Flame for this is to write down your new role, how you want others to perceive you and what you want to achieve in this new job.

An appropriate image for promotion is a tree. You are 'reaching up' and 'branching out'. This works well as a visualisation or by using a drawing of a tree. Create or find one with visible roots as these represent your foundations, your core values, skills and talents. Let your roots hold your ego in check whilst supporting your growth and you will find that others will respond to you accordingly.

You may like to see your name written on the tree trunk. The lower branches represent your training and experience up to this point.

Imagine or colour your tree in violet, write your new tasks on the new higher branches, adding words such as 'fulfilment', 'achievement' or 'respect'. Words that are suitable for your job may just come to your mind; add them in if they feel right to you. This helps you remain true to yourself; it is your role that is changing, not who you are.

If you want something more tangible you could wear or carry Violet Flame crystals to help you through the transition.

Moving sideways...

Restructures

These are often changes that are not of your choosing and are therefore much harder to accept and adapt to.

David worked at an advertising agency in London as part of the creative design team. Restructuring of the agency meant that a different department took on the art work whilst David was asked to write copy and slogans etc. Having previously worked on whole projects from start to finish he found it incredibly frustrating and annoying to pass over the responsibility for the visual concepts to others who he felt did not have adequate experience. This sometimes resulted in a mismatch of images and words that he felt did not produce the most effective advertisements.

David used the infinity symbol (figure of eight) exercise to bring a sense of unity to the projects he worked on. Because he was creative and artistic he formed a complete design based on the symbol, which ended up looking rather like a violet flower with many petals. In each campaign he used the design as a template and wrote key words in some of the 'loops' or petals of the symbol. In others he copied and pasted some of the images in miniature that were being used. He found this technique of combining the words and images worked well.

He applied this symbol in multiple shades of violet and purple to the entire agency, overlapping many layers and aspects of their work, bringing it all to a focus in the centre. He printed off several copies and displayed them all around the agency.

After a while he was asked to oversee both departments, thus bringing back the unity that had been lacking.

The more elaborate you make your design and the more energy that goes in to it, the more power there is to create the changes you intend.

Many other methods of working with the Violet Flame will ease the uncertainty and anxiety associated with this type of change. It often helps to write down your feelings and work with the Violet Flame to transmute the fear of the unknown and change your perceptions. You can then see the positive opportunities that can arise as a result of change and look beyond this present situation.

Moving out...

Redundancy

The emotions that follow redundancy are much like those following the end of a relationship, and you need to go through the process of grieving before you can move on. Feeling helpless, unwanted or not good enough will be covered later in the book. For now we will focus on using the Violet Flame to work through the stages of emotions and experiences that redundancy can trigger.

In simple terms these stages are described as: denial, anger, barter, depression and finally acceptance.

The subheadings could read:

◆ Denial – 'It's not happening', 'if I ignore it, it won't happen', 'it doesn't apply to me'.
◆ Anger – 'How dare you', 'you can't do this to me', 'after all I've done for you'.
◆ Barter – 'If I work harder can I keep my job?', 'if I have less pay can I stay?'
◆ Depression – 'I'm not worth caring about', 'there is nothing left to look forward to', 'why should I bother?'
◆ Acceptance – 'It's happened and I can deal with it', 'it's time to move on'.

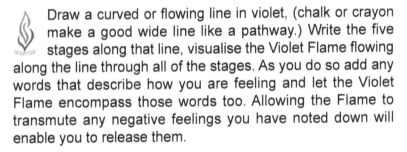 Draw a curved or flowing line in violet, (chalk or crayon make a good wide line like a pathway.) Write the five stages along that line, visualise the Violet Flame flowing along the line through all of the stages. As you do so add any words that describe how you are feeling and let the Violet Flame encompass those words too. Allowing the Flame to transmute any negative feelings you have noted down will enable you to release them.

Or you can imagine yourself walking along that line like a path in front of you that is set with Violet Flames which spark in to life with every step you take. As each flame ignites, breathe in the Violet Light and breathe out the negative emotions. You may feel it draw up through your feet, cleansing and re-energising as it rises through you. No matter where you start on the path the Violet Flame will help you reach the final stage of acceptance.

Terry was made redundant from his job as a printer after eighteen years. Although many others were made redundant at the same time and he was not singled out, he held on to the anger of losing his job for a long time. He blamed every-body from the bosses of the company to the banks who cancelled the firm's overdraft facility, even the government for the recession. The focus of most of his anger was directed at his immediate manager who had the unenviable task of informing him of his redundancy. No amount of severance pay could have eased the hurt he felt in being 'discarded', left for scrap after years and years of loyal service. He ranted to his friends and family continually.

His wife Julie had thankfully learnt of the Violet Flame and was able to firstly shield herself from absorbing his anger. She kept the Violet Flame built up in her energy field with the outside golden shell shiny and reflective. Realising that her husband was not having any success getting a new job because he was trapped in the 'anger' phase of the process, she was aware that the possibility of him becoming depressed was very likely. In order to help him move through the cycle to the 'acceptance' phase and forgive his manager she placed sugilite crystals (for forgiveness) under his pillow, in his drinking water, and kept one with his photograph in her sacred space (which was a violet coloured box she kept to herself).

Terry did not support his wife's interests or beliefs and would not have normally accepted the Violet Flame but she intuitively felt assured that his Higher Self welcomed the help. The sugilite helped to take the focus off his manager until the anger was contained more within himself. At this stage his wife continually visualised him with Violet Flame spheres, like water bombs, exploding all over him, surrounding him with Violet Light. For good measure, in desperation, she repeated a daily affirmation to release him from the anger.

For a long while the redundancy did affect his self esteem so his wife continued to hold him in the Violet Flame until he eventually was able to find re-employment. Years later he discussed this time with her and she was able to tell him of the Violet Flame and how it had helped him which he accepted without dismissing it as mumbo jumbo.

Farewell and Goodbye!

Retirement

Even when retirement is looked forward to, maybe days crossed off the calendar until retirement date, it still takes some adjustment to a different way of life. The Violet Flame can help change your perception of something ending to something starting. The gift of time is very precious to pursue hobbies, interests, and even holidays that were not possible whilst working. The issue of your role or place at work and at home has to change and many people feel removed from what has identified them in the past. It is never as easy as it sounds to adapt to having time on your hands. Feeling perhaps unfulfilled or a loss of purpose is quite common. Relationships at home often change when one partner retires.

When my own father retired there were many changes at home. He was a Wing Commander in the RAF, used to being in a position of authority, respected and obeyed but very popular. He retired relatively young having had a dangerous job as a test pilot so retirement was a complete change and tough adjustment from his working life. Coming home to two teenage daughters probably didn't help! The change of coming from a life of order and control to a life of unpredictability and disorder was a shock. Had I known about the Violet Flame then I am sure I could have helped our whole family to adjust, particularly for my mother trying to keep the peace. I would have anchored the Violet Flame in the centre of our house so that all of us could have lived within the energy of transformation to ensure a smooth and harmonious atmosphere.

By standing in the centre of the home and building the Violet Flame within myself I would have set the intent by visualisation of a recess in the floor like a silver dish with the Violet Flame burning brightly there, its glow filling the house. Alternatively I could have set the Violet Flame alight within the foundations or the cavity walls wherever felt most appropriate and effective. By filling the home with Violet Light the dynamics of the family unit would have settled more quickly than they did.

If you find yourself in a family unit or couple where one member has retired and the balance of relationships has been affected, another method could be to have a photograph of the people involved and lay a crystal mandala over it, perhaps as simple as a circle to hold the energy intact.

"Every book lets you peek into a different life"
– Author unknown

Chris had been a librarian since leaving school; she loved being in a position to inspire children to read and learn from books, stretching their imagination and honouring the time given to the whole experience of reading. She was single, with no family and was not looking forward to her retirement until she found a small violet coloured book in the 'Mind, Body, Spirit' section of the library. She read about the Violet Flame and how it can help you to change your life.

Knowing that I work with the Violet Flame, she asked me for any other ways by which she could change her perception as it was really getting her down. She wrote down what she thought retirement would mean to her: loneliness and isolation, feeling a loss of purpose and the fact that she would miss all the people who came in to the library, particularly the children. She started to see these misgivings change gradually with use of the Violet Flame, as other possibilities came to her mind. She could volunteer at the local hospital or church, both of which had a small library, and help neighbours' children with their reading and homework.

She came to view her retirement in a different light. By creating her future within the Violet Flame, the transition was so smooth that by the time she retired she was in such demand that she could never imagine feeling isolated, lonely or worthless.

CHAPTER 7

Summary

Job and career matters

- The Violet Flame can help you find the right job that suits your skills, talents and interests.

Self-employed:

- Infuse your advertising with Violet Flame energy for the maximum effect in attracting customers or clients.

- Hold the Violet Flame within you so that you can change from one role to another with ease.

- If doubts arise as to whether you have done the right thing, transmute them in the Violet Flame for future confidence.

- The Violet Flame can lessen any stress and frustration, clearing the way for a positive solution.

- Time and workload can be managed more effectively if your daily tasks are done within the Violet Flame.

- Major disputes can be tackled with the Violet Flame. There are usually three aspects to consider: clearing away negativity, protecting yourself and your workplace, focusing on the positive outcome.

In employment:

- When looking for employment use the Violet Flame to ensure your application is received and looked at in a favourable light.

- Any disappointment caused by rejections can be transmuted within the Violet Flame, helping you to remain positive.

- Along with the usual preparations for an interview, strengthen the Violet Flame within you.

- Take the Violet Flame into your new work environment. Other people will respond to the energy without knowing why.

- Violet Flame aura sprays can help greatly with stress at work, keeping the atmosphere clear and positive.

- Use the Violet Flame to transmute any anger or frustrations on the way home from work as a way to 'switch off' from the day, so that your free time is 'free'.

- Use the Violet Flame to balance an uneven distribution of workload.

- Feeling overworked for any reason can be exhausting. To boost your own energy levels, regularly maintain the Violet Flame within you and protect the outer edge of your aura.

- You can adapt to any changes at work easily with the Violet Flame. Your role may change, but not who you are.

- It may help to write down your feelings, and transmute any uncertainty or anxiety in the Violet Flame, so that you can see positive opportunities ahead.

- The Violet Flame can help you to work through the stages of emotions and experiences that redundancy can trigger.

- When you retire, the Violet Flame can help change your perception from 'something ending', to beginning 'a new way of life'.

CHAPTER 8

HEALTH AND WELLBEING

When you work with the Violet Flame on a regular basis its energy will build up inside you and radiate out to others, even if you are not a healer. Just by being close to someone who carries that energy will have an effect on the way you feel; for example, when you hug someone who carries the Violet Flame within them, all feels right with the world, worries and concerns seem to melt away and you are left feeling refreshed and recharged. I have often been told my hugs have this effect on the friends and people I work with. This in no way depletes my energy, in fact unless somebody mentions it, or responds with a sigh or a smile I am not aware of any change taking place. It just happens naturally with no conscious thought on my part because I live my life in the Violet Flame; it is just part of who I am. It's a nice, gentle way of helping those who have no understanding or interest in this matter and I've seen people respond many times without knowing why.

Keeping the energy flowing...

You will find your general health will improve with regular use of the Violet Flame. The flow of energy throughout our bodies needs to be smooth in order for us to be well. When that energy flow is blocked or interrupted we suffer pain or illness, usually at the point where the blockage occurs. This, our life-force energy, flows along invisible lines called meridians and they pass through seven major centres, at certain points of our body. These are our chakras; they can quite easily become blocked!

The Violet Flame helps to keep the energy moving through the body so that it becomes less easy for any illness, injury or dis-ease to take a hold. Although the Violet Flame in itself is not a cure for all conditions it certainly helps to maintain good health. It can be used in quite specific ways to improve our health and wellbeing whether physical, emotional or mental.

Treat the cause not just the symptom

There are frequently non-physical causes of health problems. Problems with the throat are often due to an inability to express yourself clearly or tell someone how you are feeling. The energy blocks there with the unspoken emotions. Problems with the feet often relate to how you stand up for yourself or whether you can move forward in your life. The energy that blocks here will certainly stop you in your tracks, but may lead to you keep tripping over, or twisting an ankle.

If you think about the common phrases and idioms we use in everyday language that relate to parts of the body this will give you a good idea of the relationship between physical effects and the possible non-physical causes.

For example:
"Keeping your head above water" shows how financial worries can be a real headache.
"The weight of the world on my shoulders" shows where we carry responsibility.
"They're a real pain in the neck" shows there is no flexibility in someone's attitude.
"It brought me to my knees" indicates shock, trauma, despair all of which create problems in the knees.

The Violet Flame can heal at the point of origin, back at the time when pain or discomfort first occurred, transmuting the shock, and any negative emotions that arose at the time. This has a 'ripple effect' through to the present time and the pain or difficulty that is being experienced will then start to heal. If you can consciously find the reason for the injury or illness the recovery will be quicker and more complete.

Of course, human beings are extremely complex, and every aspect of life affects us in one way or another, often all at the same time, until it may be hard to distinguish what is emotional, what is mental and what has triggered any specific physical condition. So do not try too hard to work it out if the answer is not apparent; it can help greatly even to place it at a moment in time, and start the healing from there. Sometimes that will cause images to come to mind and intuitively the cause may be known.

Ouch! That hurts!

Physical injury or illness

To use the Violet Flame to help heal a physical injury you could replay the incident in your mind of when the injury occurred. Pay attention to as much detail as you can; be aware of your thoughts and feelings at the time and visualise yourself with the Violet Flame burning brightly at your heart, spreading through your entire body, focusing its strength on the point of injury. Imagine seeing the Violet Flame in and around that area in the days and weeks afterwards until it has healed. You could also regularly imagine a violet coloured bandage around it.

Jessie, who is in her early sixties with a large family and young grandchildren, had a series of small slips and trips, each one not enough to be classed as an accident but combined they had weakened her lower back causing her considerable pain. She couldn't stand for more than a few minutes and she couldn't sleep. The painkillers she had been prescribed did not seem to help so she asked me what else she could do to enhance the physiotherapy treatment she was receiving. Talking to her about her family and asking what support they gave her it was not surprising that she reluctantly told me "None". The lower back very often relates to giving and receiving generally, and particularly the support you receive from family, friends and work colleagues. The lack of support meant that her back was not healing as it could. I worked on her physical back with the Violet Flame, igniting the spark of it at her coccyx and I asked her to visualise daily Violet Flames flickering up her spine, focusing on where the pain was worse, and on the glow of the Violet Flame spreading out through her muscles and across her lower back. I asked her to write down why she feels she can not ask for help from her family, why she wants to do everything for them, receiving little in return. I asked her to b honest and told her that she need not share this with me so that she could keep it private. We folded the paper and burnt it in the flame of a violet candle. As it burnt she repeated:

"I release all restrictions that stop me from accepting support from my family. I can now ask for and accept their help and support."

She repeated this as often as she could throughout the days that followed until she found she was able to ask for some help which her family gladly gave. Her family were surprised as they had always assumed she didn't need any help. Within a few weeks her back was much improved.

Many years ago I was diagnosed with type two diabetes and since working with the Violet Flame I have had none of the associated problems. Along with following dietary advice and medication, I wrote myself an affirmation that the diabetes would not adversely affect my life and the Violet Flame would transmute any negativity that had triggered it. It had been a time in my life when the 'sweetness' had gone and I was consumed with bitterness. The Violet Flame sorted that out too!

I think... therefore I am

Mental wellbeing

Medically diagnosed mental health issues will not be covered here but the importance of our mental wellbeing should not be overlooked as thoughts are the foundation of health and healing.

Every action starts with a thought. Whether that thought is positive or negative is going to determine the outcome of the action. In order to live a positive, strong and healthy life you need to start with positive, strong and healthy thoughts. When negative thoughts adversely affect you or your life the hardest part is becoming aware of them and actually wanting to change them. It is too easy to remain stuck with old patterns and habits that you may have grown up with, rather than change the way you think. There are many books on the market about positive thinking; it is a well recognised approach to healing. The Violet Flame is a very useful tool to change your thoughts from negative to positive and tackle those issues that hold you back in life such as low self-esteem.

Even the most positive person has some negative thoughts – this is normal and natural. However, if negative thoughts predominate in any area or aspect of your life, problems can arise. Likewise if you are too controlling of your thoughts, constantly forcing yourself to focus only on the positive, you allow no room in your mind for free thinking. Freedom of thought encourages inspiration and new ideas, enabling you to look at your health and wellbeing in a totally holistic way. Balance is required and the Violet Flame is the easiest way to achieve that.

Who? Me?

Confidence and self-esteem

Low self-esteem is rooted in your belief system; what you believe of yourself and how you believe others see you are often learned in childhood. It can affect your perception of many different areas of your life, for example your appearance, capabilities, personal worth, even your future choices.

Claire worked in a call centre at an insurance company where she was successful in her sales role, as she had a great gift for putting people at ease. She also answered the firm's Customer Services calls where she was often asked for by name. When she was offered promotion to a job where she would be meeting customers face to face her immediate reaction was to decline as she thought that her looks would put people off. She told me that she had chosen a career out of the public view because she thought she was ugly and that she would not be taken seriously with her bright red hair. It turned out that she had been teased as a child and her self-esteem badly damaged.

I asked her to describe the image she had of herself, and wrote that down in violet, putting it away in a violet coloured box file.

When she was completely relaxed, I asked her to describe her self-esteem as if it were a tangible object. What did it look like (colour, size, shape)? Where did she keep it? Can she take it out of her body so that she could look at it objectively? Her automatic response was that she didn't know what it looked like but she kept it in a pink handbag! She thought it might be a small pink handbag that she had been given as a child at about the same time she was being teased. I asked her to visualise a spark of Violet Flame dropping into it. I told her to look inside the handbag and see it grow into a strong flame, gradually filling the bag with Violet Light and feeling that light radiate out all around her, letting the energy of the Violet Flame transmute all her poor self-image until she was able to close the handbag. She said the bag simply disappeared.

She cried as she thought of all the years her low self-esteem had held her back from jobs, relationships and general confidence. This then spurred her on to seek counselling, as it was clearly a very deep-seated issue that she had struggled with for so long.

We worked out a decree and affirmation for her to repeat as often as possible to help increase her confidence:

"The Violet Flame changes the negative image I hold, I see myself now as bright, vibrant and bold."

"I am caring, professional and good at my job; I will succeed at whatever I do."

She repeated them firstly to herself, then aloud and in time she could say them whilst looking at herself in the mirror.

I heard from her several weeks later that she had accepted the promotion, but was still receiving counselling. Some months later we met and I read out her original description of herself, she laughed and said:
"That's not me."
She told me that she still uses Violet Flame affirmations to help her get through tough times, whenever her confidence is challenged.

But I've always done it this way!

Changing Patterns of Behaviours

When you recognise patterns of behaviour that are at best not productive and at worst self-destructive you can change them with the Violet Flame. Some of these patterns could include yo-yo dieting, destructive relationships, or an over-reliance on anything or anyone other than yourself.

In some instances, repeating patterns of learnt behaviour is a good thing. You would want to repeat the response to potential danger: for example, if something is hot you know through experience not to touch it.

Sometimes these patterns or habits can become disconnected from the situation that triggered the response in the first place. Losing weight for a special occasion feels wonderful and is a credit to willpower. However, if it is all put back on afterwards that can engender feelings of guilt, disappointment and anger with oneself. Struggling then to lose the re-gained weight has no connection to the original intent; so the cycle can continue with your weight going up and down like a yo-yo. Recognising these habits that are repeated without purpose or value is the first step to being able to change them.

Opportunities come up in life for you to learn and grow from. If we do not 'get it' the first time, the opportunity will arise again and again until we do! How we respond to situations is more important than the situation itself. Repeating patterns does not give you new ways to deal with situations or expand your experiences. By reacting in a different way each time a situation repeats you eventually learn which way was the best. This is how you grow and can move on to new experiences.

James was a university lecturer, a good friend of mine, gay, in his mid-forties with a string of unsuccessful relationships behind him. Having just met a new man called Max, he had high hopes of this relationship and could not wait to tell me all about him. This seemed like a good opportunity for me to urge him to look at the patterns he had repeated in the past and suggest that maybe this time he would like to break that unsuccessful pattern. He was surprised when I pointed out the similarities in his past relationships: that however different his partners had been, the actual relationships had all followed a similar course; that in fact he was creating the same scenarios time after time. In trying to be and do every-thing for his partner he was dominating every aspect, almost mothering and smothering them. As one of life's givers he found it hard to know when to stop. Despite being attracted to seemingly independent, outgoing men, over time with his constant 'help' they became reliant and dependent on him until he lost interest and their neediness infuriated him.

We spent one afternoon on his computer, going through photographs of his previous partners. We selected images of him with each them, and using the edit facility, we changed the overall colour to violet. We stored those in a file on his desktop named 'previous relationships' and suggested that every time he turned the computer on and saw the icon for that file, he visualised the Violet Flame encompassing those relationships. He opened up a new document, inserted a violet border pattern and wrote Max's full name in violet text with the words "We give and receive in equal amounts". This denoted the new pattern, for his new relationship, and this he stored in another file named 'new relationship'.

He was reminded of his intent to change the pattern of his relationships every time he turned the computer on and so was able to stop himself slipping back in to his old patterns. Sadly, Max wasn't 'The One' either, perhaps as we had rewritten the intent after they had started seeing each other, so we looked at attracting the right relationship from the start, and I am happy to say that is still working – James is settled and happy in a mutually supportive relationship.

I want to give up, but how?

Changing Habits

We all have habits of one sort or another, repetitive actions that we do without thinking. Most are harmless and even helpful, providing order in our lives, but if these become obsessive or addictive they can be disruptive and even destructive. Habits can be patterns that repeat over long periods of time and these are harder to break than something that has just become a habit for a short while. In particular, habits of dieting fall in to this category, often resulting in weight going up and down like a yo-yo.

I recognised this in myself over many years and decided to use the Violet Flame to let my body find its own balance. I looked back to when I had first started crash dieting as a teenager. I wanted to emulate the thin models on the pages of magazines and to lose my puppy fat so that I could fit in with my older sister's friends. I recognised that this was the start of feeling if I was slim I would be more attractive and if I was more attractive I would be happier, regardless of what sort of person I am.

I made a conscious choice to change. I threw away my scales and used the Violet Flame daily to realign my inner and outer self. The Violet Flame transmuted my fear of being fat which in turn stopped me crash dieting which I had done on many occasions, trying every new fad going to lose weight quickly. I also used it to boost my confidence and stop my habit of feeling sorry for myself which is what led to the overeating. I visualised reigniting the spark within me every morning and letting the Violet Light fill my physical body, pushing it out through my chakras, back and front, so that the Violet Flame energy filled my aura within the gold protective outer shell. My inner self and my outer image became one. I saw myself for who I am, not just for what I look like.

When others started to notice the change in me and see who I am rather than the image I portrayed, I felt much more comfortable with myself and stopped dieting. Although not the slimmest I have been, my weight is stable and I am healthy.

The Violet Flame has now become my habit and I feel fantastic!

Heart and mind

Emotional balance

Children are very heart-based; they think of it as the centre of their being. As we grow older our decisions are often made using our mind not our heart and we lose that connection. We leave our hearts vulnerable and exposed to hurt and disappointment, creating blockages and disconnection between the chakras. Perhaps the most common reason for emotional imbalance is because our heart and mind are in conflict, telling us different things. We need to listen to both, not one or the other. The Violet Flame can bring these two back into alignment helping us to deal with life's shocks and knocks.

Exercise to reconnect your heart and mind:

Focusing the Violet Flame midway between the two at the throat chakra is most easily done by using the voice, so I would recommend a chant. To help align your heart and mind, sit in an upright chair. You may like to play some gentle background music and, after taking a few deep breaths, quietly and slowly repeat the following mantra in a monotone voice: (It sounds just as it is written)

"Om Mani Padme Hum"

This is the mantra of Kuan Yin. It is translated in several ways, but the most pertinent here is: *'The Jewel of the mind has reached the Lotus of the heart'*.

The volume of any chant should build as you continue to repeat the words without a break between repetitions, taking a breath whenever you need to. Keep going as long as you like. You may also like to visualise the Violet Flame spreading up into your mind and down to your heart so the glow envelops both.

Using the Violet Flame in this way will bring your heart and mind back into alignment and help you to restore balance in your life.

It's all in the mind... or is it?

Fear and Phobias

Fears and phobias are felt very strongly as an emotional reaction but do they spring from the mind or the heart or from somewhere in between? Wherever fears and phobias stem from, sometimes bad childhood experiences and sometime previous lifetimes, the Violet Flame can help to release them.

Sue had a fear of flying that was stopping her going on holiday with her family. They were becoming infuriated with her as her husband had booked a trip as her fiftieth birthday treat and she had simply said she could not go. It was one of her children who asked if I could help and Sue was very willing to try anything to overcome this fear once and for all. This did take several sessions as we needed to find the root cause of her fear and transmute it from there. It transpired that when she was a child her elder brother had dangled her out of an upstairs window by her ankles because she had broken something of his. Thereafter he threatened to do it again whenever she annoyed him. So the fear had built up over a long time and, even though she had tried to block the original incident from her mind, she felt the same fear whenever she could see the ground from a height or there was a possibility of that happening, hence her fear of flying. Apart from this she grew up to be quite a tough and feisty lady, never having told her family of her fear.

Acknowledging the cause of her fear of flying, she was able leave it in her childhood and deal solely with the effects of her traumatic experience. She still dearly loved her brother and felt no anger towards him, as he had been a great help and very protective of her as they reached adulthood.

Having talked over several different method options we decided that I would talk her through a visualisation as if she was going on holiday with her family, through each stage of the journey. We went through the process of igniting the Violet Flame within her, filling her aura and placing a golden shield around her and then I started to talk her through packing her cases, getting in to the taxi, making her way to the airport, still always surrounded by the energy of the Violet Flame. The first time we did this she only got as far as getting into the taxi; when the doors shut, she panicked. I told her to open her eyes and we again went through the process of building the Violet Flame within and around her. The second time we made it to the airport. We continued this process over several sessions until she could visualise getting through the entire journey including the flight home. I spoke to her the night before they left on holiday and she said she felt very calm because she had gone over it so many times in her mind with the Violet Flame to transmute the fear. The next time I heard from her was a postcard from Spain simply saying "Sat by the window, no alcohol or drugs!"

The causes of fear are not always rooted in some past event or a previous lifetime. Fear of the unknown is well recognised. Understanding the possibility of danger can, in itself, trigger a fear so intense that physical wellbeing can suffer as a result.

Some years ago a good friend of mine was undergoing tests for cancer. Quite naturally the anxiety was taking its toll. With his mind full of 'What if it is cancer?' 'How will my family cope if I'm not able to work, or not even here?' and 'I've still got things I want to do and achieve,' his energy levels were plummeting and his general wellbeing was suffering. I could see his health deteriorating just with the stress of worrying what might happen, leaving him no strength to cope with the results should they be cancer. I urged him to spend some time each day focusing on the Violet Flame, and every time the fears intruded into his thoughts, to imagine a violet coloured cloud in front of his face absorbing all the negative thoughts from his mind. I told him to breathe in Violet Light, breathing out all the dread and fear as grey light, until he was breathing the Violet Light both in and out.

By the time the results of his tests arrived he was prepared to face the outcome with positive energy, a strong way of coping with the stress and I am happy to say, he is still with us!

It doesn't make any sense!

Phobias

Phobias are often irrational, extreme fears that cannot usually be traced back to a previous incident or experience. Some are well known and documented such as claustrophobia, agoraphobia, arachnophobia and some are more unusual such as an irrational fear of striped patterns or even the most bizarre I heard of: Morris dancers.

I would suggest that you prepare a crystal mandala using any of the crystals already mentioned that carry the energy of the Violet Flame, in whatever pattern appeals to you. Place within it something that represents your phobia; for example a plain black box if you are dealing with claustrophobia, a plastic spider, or a piece of striped material, whatever for you provokes the emotional feeling of panic. Just a plain circle of crystals works very well; the energy of them focuses in to the centre and is directed towards the object of your phobia. Look at the item within the mandala daily and repeat aloud:

"I release my phobia of...... (insert phobia) to the crystals of the Violet Flame," until you can look at the object without fear or panic.

Following on from this, when you are ready to, place the crystals in the same pattern around a chair, sit on the chair and hold the object that represents your phobia. Now close your eyes, take a few deep breaths, ground yourself, feel the protection of the crystals around you, know that you are safe and secure, and visualise yourself in the situation that has previously induced the feeling of panic. Pay attention to your breathing and feel with every breath that you are drawing in the energy of the crystals, bringing the Violet Flame to transmute your fear and panic. Repeat aloud:

"I release my phobia of... (insert phobia) to the crystals of the Violet Flame," until you can visualise being in that situation without fear or panic.

Repeat this as often as necessary until the fear subsides. Remember to cleanse your crystals after you have finished using them, and thank them for their part in transmuting your phobia. (Violet Flame crystals and cleansing methods are given in chapter 4.)

If your phobia is severe, this practice will enhance any other therapy you may be utilising to tackle the problem. It is often advisable to have a friend or family member with you to help you anyway.

Heart to heart

Mending a broken heart

A broken heart really hurts! It can feel like a physical pain in your solar plexus; as if punched by a champion boxer, it can knock the wind out of you and make you physically sick. After the initial reaction the pain seems to move up to your heart chakra and remain like a constant ache which can sharpen with thoughts of whatever or whoever caused your heart to break. Crying is not enough to alleviate extreme heart ache; you feel you will never get over it.

Paula was in her late forties, had been married to Scott for more than twenty years and they had a good lifestyle. Two of their children had already left home and the youngest was just about to leave for university. Scott had been having an affair very discreetly for several years, waiting for the children to all leave home before moving to live with his mistress. Paula had no idea of his infidelity and so it dropped as a bombshell when she discovered the truth. When she confronted him, and he did not deny it, the hurt and betrayal she felt at having been deceived for so long was unbearable and the pain she felt was very real.

She turned to a spiritual medium she knew for help and guidance and the medium recommended her to work with the Violet Flame. She contacted me and said:

"My heart's broken; it hurts so much, what can I do?"

From personal experience, I knew this was going to be a long process and the first thing to do would be to help her feel safe and protected. When she came to me, we worked on strengthening the shell around her aura, filling her entire energy field with the Violet Flame. I talked her through a meditation going to the Violet Flame Temple for healing and recorded it so she could listen to it at home whenever she felt she needed to. (You will find this meditation in the Healing chapter that follows). She found this very helpful emotionally and the physical pain lessened to what she described as a dull ache which felt heavy and solid in her chest. She was also feeling that she would never be able to trust anyone again and so we worked with the image of her heart, closed in and contained like a nut in its shell. I told her that this was fine for a while, a protective layer around her heart, and when she was ready she could break the shell and open her heart again.

At this point in her life she decided to start painting again, which she had not done since the children were young. She brought a painting round to show me which was an emotional expression of the pain and anguish that she felt. She said that she had found it a great help to pour out her feelings in this way. We rolled the painting up loosely, tied it with some violet coloured ribbon and asked Kuan Yin to help ease the pain that was expressed in the painting. Paula took it home with her and every day asked Kuan Yin to continue bringing the Violet Flame to her painting. Some weeks later, without unwrapping the first one, she painted a new picture depicting her feelings as she felt they had changed. When we compared the two, the second showed slightly brighter colours and a lighter mood. Her emotions and her stability were very up and down for many months as the practicalities of the changes to her life were sorted out. She continued painting and some of them she referred to as her 'heart paintings'. By her fifth 'heart painting' she was ready to crack open the nut.

She practised a daily visualisation; filling the shell with Violet Flame energy until, bit by bit, she started to see the shell crack as the light emitted from it.

Paula became very confident in using the Violet Flame in all sorts of creative ways and when I saw her many years later she was working on a series of paintings inspired by its trans-formational energy. She was planning an exhibition of her work and was very excited at the prospect.

Sometimes it takes what seems like a disaster at the time to push us in another direction or to fulfil us in a way we had not planned. I was so happy to see that Paula had used her own gifts and talents, interacting with the Violet Flame, to bring about such positive change in her life. She said she felt inspired by working with Lady Portia for justice, truth and balance and Saint Germain for freedom from any painful memories.

Gone... but not forgotten

Bereavement

The death or loss of a loved one is one of the main disruptions to your emotional balance; it throws everything into chaos. It is widely acknowledged as the most stressful situation you will ever have to deal with and often raises the issue of your own mortality. This is the one thing that is inevitable in all our lives and the one thing most people dread.

The Violet Flame ensures an easier and more peaceful transi-tion through what can be a very difficult time for all concerned, no matter whether it is sudden or a long drawn out process.

Passing peacefully

We all want a peaceful transition into the realm of Spirit and there are ways in which we can ease the journey. There is often a sense of helplessness which accompanies the gradual demise and ultimate loss of a loved one. As they near the end of their life, you can use the Violet Flame in any way you choose to help them. It can only work for the Highest Good, so you are merely enhancing the natural energy that they will pass through, not rushing them on their way.

Working with the Violet Flame at this time gives you a sense of purpose and a very real ability to help. This eases any feelings of guilt; such as wondering if you could have done more, and helps you through your grief, ultimately to accept their passing, peacefully.

> It took nearly a year for my sister to die of cancer; watching her steady decline and suffering meant that the grief started long before she actually died. I missed the person she had been and still looked for her in the physical body that I visited in the hospice. She had been so full of life that it was hard to see that taken away from her and to see her still alive but with no life. At the time I knew nothing of the Violet Flame and felt helpless, which made matters worse. It was only once she had gone that I was able to recall happy memories of how she had been before she had cancer. The grief was totally different before and after.

> Likewise with my father, watching the strong man I knew and had loved all my life become helpless and lose his dignity was far more painful than his actual passing. When he died I felt relief that he was no longer suffering and, having been able to teach him about the Violet Flame and use it together to ease his passing, the grief I felt was peaceful and almost joyful.

It certainly helps whenever you are with the person to build the Violet Flame within you and feel it expanding through you and out through your aura so when you are with them the Violet

Flame encompasses them too. It transmutes any negativity and fears around their passing and helps them to prepare.

 When the time for them to pass is close, visualise a tunnel of Violet Light reaching up from them to the bright light of Spirit, opening up a passage through which their spirit can travel. It also enables close family members or friends who have previously passed to approach more easily through that vibration of energy. You are not speeding up the process, for they will only go when they are ready and without it their deceased loved ones will still draw near at the end, but the Violet Flame will make that transition smoother and less fearful for the individual. You can repeat this visualisation as often as you feel is appropriate until they have passed from this physical life.

Out of the blue!

Suddenly gone

If someone dies suddenly the Violet Flame can help with the shock as well as the grief.

Geoff's heart attack was so massive and instant that he knew nothing about it. He was a hard-working man who had always provided well for his wife and children. Stella was devastated when Geoff's boss broke the news to her. There had been no time for goodbyes and her thoughts went back to when he had left for work that morning, what had been said and the last image she had of him and then the shock hit her. Thankfully she had no worries financially and his affairs were all in order so she could focus on their children, supporting them through their grief without giving in to her own. So it was many months later that she felt herself cracking under the strain of rebuilding their lives and came to ask for help. I could see the shock was still present within her and we dealt with that first. It took several very emotional sessions working with the Violet Flame to transmute that energy. We went through all the methods as she was desperate to try everything she could to get over this. She found writing down her feelings and burning them in the flame of a violet candle was the most helpful as it released a lot of anger that she had held back from showing in front of the children.

As the shock healed she was able to let go and grieve. She started to become very interested in the healing power of crystals and bought several to place around the home. She gave an amethyst to each of her children, and also taught them several ways of using the Violet Flame by which they could deal with their emotions – methods which stood them in good stead as they grew up. One of them enjoyed drawing so placed a photograph of her father in a frame that she had decorated herself with patterns of Violet Flames. She also created several different Violet Flame mandalas to hang on the wall in her bedroom.

The shock of a sudden passing is also absorbed by the spirit or soul of the person who has passed. The section on sending distance healing will also cover sending it to a spirit or soul who has passed from this life.

Tears fill the void, but when tears dry, there is still the void

Dealing with grief

However they pass, and whatever your personal relationship or feelings towards the person, their passing will inevitably unsettle your emotions and leave a gap in your life. Grief is different for everyone; it is a very personal experience but the Violet Flame can help greatly to ease the pain and sadness. Have you ever heard someone wish they'd had a chance to say goodbye to a relative or friend before they passed over to Spirit? Or wish they'd said something meaningful in those last days, or hours of life? One of the most dreadful experiences must be the loss of a child, but remember they all pass through Violet Light on their way between worlds; it has no boundaries across Time or Space, and so we can still reach their energy using that. Our messages sent through the Violet Flame will reach them.

People tend to feel loss as a hole or a gap in their life that can be filled with the Violet Flame, or it is felt as a rock or boulder that weighs them down with grief and the Violet Flame can help lighten that load.

Visualise the hole or gap left as a real place within your physical body, like a secret cave within your heart. Just like we would light a candle for a person who has passed, light a Violet Flame within your secret cave and imagine it filling with Violet Light, like a shrine to the person who has passed. Whenever you think of them, think of that little flame reigniting and the glow building up. It is a place for all your sadness and grief to go. Whatever emotions you feel, whether anger, guilt, regret, yearning, loneliness or even relief, pour those emotions into your cave and let the Violet Flame transmute them.

In time the difficult feelings will ease and happier memories will surface to fill that space within you. Eventually you may like to visualise it as a real cave, filled with Violet Flame candles; it may be a place where you can go and sit with them, chat to them, share memories and feelings with them whilst surrounded by the violet glow.

I remember being told once by a lady very dear to me that on the loss of her husband it had felt like a great weight dropped into her lap like a boulder. She was only four foot ten inches but had the strength to carry that weight of her grief. When I saw her a couple of years after her husband had passed she said to me:

"You know, Hilary, people used to say to me that time would take away the pain and the weight of this grief. It doesn't ever really go though. It just becomes a little easier to carry with time."

I wish I had been able to introduce her to the Violet Flame and show her ways of using it to lighten her load.

I think with hindsight that a mantra would have been most appropriate for her to work with on a daily basis. I would have suggested that she take in a deep breath of Violet Light and recite in her mind the first line as she breathes in and the second line breathing out, repeated three times.

"The Violet Flame lightens the weight of my grief.
It connects our souls forever.'

With each breath she would have been releasing the grief and the weight of her emotions, filling her body with Violet Flame energy and strengthening that connection with her husband. They were happily reunited some years later.

CHAPTER 8

Summary

Health and wellbeing

- There are frequently non-physical causes of health problems. Use the Violet Flame to treat the cause not just the symptoms.

- The Violet Flame will help heal a physical injury or illness.

- Our mental wellbeing should not be overlooked. Positive, strong and healthy thoughts lead to a positive, strong and healthy life. The Violet Flame helps you to achieve this.

- Used regularly the Violet Flame can help increase confidence and self esteem.

- As a transformational energy, the Violet Flame can be used to transform any negative behaviour patterns.

- Even long term habits can be changed to increase health and wellbeing. Make the Violet Flame your habit!

- The Violet Flame can reconnect your heart and mind to restore emotional balance in your life.

- Fears and phobias can be released and overcome within the Violet Flame.

- The Violet Flame can help you to recover from the most painful experiences, enabling you to see a brighter future.

- You can use the Violet Flame to ease someone else's passing from this life.

- If someone dies suddenly the Violet Flame can help with the shock as well as the grief of those left behind.

- The Violet Flame will help to ease the pain and sense of loss caused by bereavement.

CHAPTER 9

HEALING

The Violet Flame can be used on its own or with any system of healing particularly hands-on healing such Reiki, Reflexology or Massage. In order to do any healing, the healer themselves must first be clear of any negativity, so the Violet Flame is an effective preparation before giving any type of treatment. It can be used for general wellbeing or for a specific purpose on yourself, others, animals, plants and the planet.

Any healing using the Violet Flame, whether for yourself or others, will only work for the Highest Good. So, if a health problem, for example, is an essential part of somebody's path or a lesson to be learnt in this lifetime the Violet Flame will work to ensure that the path is smoother and the lessons will be learnt perhaps more quickly, but it may not result in a physical cure. So it is not a 'quick fix' or a 'cure all' for all health issues; some have to be worked through and experienced. The Violet Flame, however, can greatly assist this process.

To use the Violet Flame for direct healing, visualise a stream of Violet Light entering your crown chakra, magnifying the Violet Light at your heart. Let it expand to fill your own body with Violet Flame energy to transmute any negativity you may hold before passing the energy out through your palm chakras. This is a similar process to Reiki and they flow together very well. It works on physical, mental and emotional aspects of life. The healing benefits will depend on how clear and focused you are, together with the natural healing abilities of the recipient.

As the Violet Flame only works for the Highest Good, there is no problem incorporating it with any mainstream treatment or medication. It is particularly complementary with the energy of a soul returning to Earth and so is wonderful to use during pregnancy.

Chakra Healing - clear the blockages

This is a very specific way to heal that 'unblocks' the chakras, encouraging a smooth flow of energy by combining the chakra colours and the Violet Flame for maximum effect. For example, a Violet Flame with its glow, or 'aura', the colour green, would transmute any negative energy that may be blocked at the heart chakra.

 If you are a healer or you feel, see, or sense energy, then you may like to try the following healing exercise using Violet Flames with chakra coloured auras:

1st / Base:
Imagine holding a small Violet Flame with a deep, ruby-red glow around it and placing it into your base chakra. Let the violet/red glow seep through to your back and the tailbone of your spine. Feel it clearing the energy there, with warmth that rises up your spine. This will transmute any feelings of being unsupported, and any fears connected with your basic needs being met. It will activate a sense of strength and courage to stand up for yourself.

2nd / Sacral:
Place a small Violet Flame with an orange glow around it at your sacral chakra and feel the energy seeping through and around your hips, and through all your lower internal organs. This will act to clear any negative self-image, and then boost morale and self esteem.

3rd / Solar Plexus:
Place a small Violet Flame with a golden yellow glow around it into your solar plexus, feel it spreading though your lower

ribcage, your upper internal organs, and digestive system, through to your spine. This will transmute any negativity held here and boost willpower and strength of purpose.

4th / Heart:
Place a small Violet Flame with a bright emerald green glow around it into your heart chakra. Feel the light expanding through your chest and upper ribcage, your lungs and heart, through to your spine. This colour combination will really ease any heartache, (and indigestion!) It induces a feeling that all is right and as it should be, that pain here will pass.

5th / Throat:
Place a small Violet Flame with a light blue glow around it into your throat chakra, and feel the cool violet and blue glow spreading through your neck, your voicebox and vocal chords, through to your spinal column where it supports your skull and across your shoulders. The combined energy of this flame will clear any 'choked up' feeling, leaving you able to speak out calmly, expressing yourself with clarity. It will also alleviate tension in the shoulders.

6th / Brow or Third Eye:
Place a small Violet Flame with a deep indigo (sapphire) glow around it into your brow/third eye chakra and feel the soothing velvety light seep through your sinuses, the space behind your eyes, into and through your brain, easing your thoughts and memories held at the back of your brain. This combined energy will clear any misconceptions and distorted memories, allowing you to see the truth and start to expand your consciousness.

7th / Crown:
Place here a small Violet Flame with a violet glow, to open your crown chakra, and seep down through the centre of your brain to the pituitary gland. Feel the combined Violet Light raise the vibrational frequency of your conscious and subconscious mind. This is the energy through which your Guides, Guardians

and all Higher Beings can resonate with you.

To use this healing for yourself, others or your pets, simply imagine holding each of these Violet Flames with their chakra coloured auras in the palms of your hands. Visualise them flickering there with their glow illuminating your skin and then place your hands on or close to the corresponding chakra. Set your intention that these chakra Violet Flames pass from your palms into the chakra, to be absorbed.

As with any healing, it must always be done with the permission of the recipient and the intent that it is for the Highest Good.

 For an emotional energy blockage, when you can't get over something and you feel it constantly, you can direct a violet/emerald ray of light to wherever the energy is blocked in the physical body. This is usually but not always at the heart; sometimes heartache can cause pain in the shoulders. Similarly, emotions that 'sicken' us or affect our digestive system can lead to pain and blocked energy in the knees. So wherever it is felt is treated as well as the point of origin, getting to both the cause and effect.

For a mental energy blockage, such as becoming overly analytical, unable to concentrate or thoughts going round in circles, use a violet/yellow or violet/gold ray of light. For example, I would place one hand aligned with the brow chakra and the other hand behind the head at the base of the skull, to direct the energy. (Yellow is the colour of the mind, thought processes and inspiration even though not the chakra colour.)

If the blockage is held through fear of basic needs not being met, or a survival threat, visualise a violet coloured flame with a ruby-red glow in each palm and direct them to the base and crown chakras at the same time. You may feel the energy passing from palm to palm through all the chakras; this would really clear the flow of energy and give you a boost!

The general principle is that to activate or energise, imagine a violet coloured flame with a bright orange/red glow around it, and to calm something down visualise a violet coloured flame with a cool, peaceful blue glow around it.

Violet Flame and Reiki

If you are a Reiki Practitioner and would like to incorporate the Violet Flame in your healing practice, they work very well together, even though they have slightly different attributes. Reiki is very calming and balancing, encouraging the smooth flow of energy throughout the body. The Violet Flame transmutes any negativity which might impede that energy flow. They combine for an efficient, general healing that can be used anytime or anywhere.

On a coach holiday to Paris we went to the Pompidou Centre which has a big underground concrete car park. This was unlit with low ceilings and was almost empty, creating a very dismal, claustrophobic atmosphere.

A lady on the coach three rows behind me was clearly feeling very uneasy as we descended level after level. I could hear her friend telling her to breathe deeply and reassuring her that it would be alright. The coach came to a stop and we all got off. At that point the driver realised that the exit on this level was locked and the lady who suffered with claustrophobia, Fiona, was beginning to hyperventilate and her eyes were starting to roll back up under her eyelids. Her friend was looking around in a panic so I went over to Fiona, placed my hand on the back of her heart chakra and silently asked the Reiki energy to flow with the Violet Flame from my hand. I talked to her to switch her focus to me rather than the situation that was causing her distress. Immediately I felt her relax and her breathing settled. I felt the Reiki and Violet Flame forming a green and purple light all around her.

Another member of the coach party found stairs, leading up to daylight. I kept my hand at her back and continued talking to her as I led her over to the stairs. Once she saw the daylight she was able to walk up the steps unaided. I kept up the combined flow of healing energy until we were out of the car park and standing on the pavement. Fiona turned to me, gave me a hug and asked:

"What was that? I felt heat going into my back that made me feel strangely calm and it was as if I suddenly knew that I would get out of this and we would be alright. All I could see was a sort of mauve colour."

I told her that it was Reiki healing combined with an energy called the Violet Flame which was probably the mauve that she saw. I told her that next time she was in a similar situation, or felt that panic rise, to remember today and know that she only has to think of that colour mauve that she saw and know that she would be alright. Even at the end of our holiday she came and hugged me again, thanked me and promised she would never forget.

Healing with Violet Flame crystals

Crystals which resonate at the same frequency as the Violet Flame are particularly effective to incorporate in any healing. They magnify or act as a focus for the Violet Flame energy. Refer to the individual crystal's healing properties (see chapter 4, or consult any book on the subject) to find the most appropriate attributes for whatever healing is required. For example, emotional healing would be heightened by the addition of Lepidolite, whereas Charoite would bring matters to the surface in order to be healed. These crystals can be placed on the body, held by the recipient or placed around the couch, to enhance any treatment.

If worn as jewellery or carried regularly, the healing properties of the crystals will be felt over a longer period of time. This is particularly effective for long term conditions and can lessen some of the debilitating side effects and complications that can occur. Alternatively keep one of the Violet Flame crystals with your medication to reduce any potentially negative side effects.

Sending distant healing

Distant healing with the Violet Flame requires the same intent and focus that any distant healing does. It can be sent to an individual person or animal, a group of people, a place, the entire world and even out into the Universe. The Violet Flame can also be sent as distant healing with or without any other healing method. Time and space are no barriers to the Violet Flame; it can be sent to anyone, anywhere, now, in the past or the future.

Remember it is a very fast or high frequency vibration of energy, so it does not need to be sent for long periods at a time; a little and often is best.

May I help you?

Before sending distant healing to anyone, you must ask if they will accept the assistance of the Violet Flame. If you are in contact with them you can ask them personally, otherwise you would need to ask them intuitively and rely on the answer from their Higher Self. If you are unsure of this, or sense no response to your request, then start to send the energy very gently and if it is not appropriate or has been rejected you will feel the energy is not flowing. Alternatively set the intent that if the Violet Flame is not required by the individual, then it goes to wherever it is needed if it is for the Highest Good. Those who have already passed over into Spirit will usually agree and welcome it for it is a highly spiritual energy.

Remember too, that you set the intent that the Violet Flame healing will be received at the most appropriate time, as it can create quite dramatic changes and people do respond to the energy of it without knowing why. So you wouldn't want to bombard them with Violet Flame if they were driving at 70mph up the motorway for example! Ask that it be received when they are at home and relaxed or asleep at night.

The Violet Flame Healing Temple

One way to send distant healing is to imagine taking someone with you to the Violet Flame Healing Temple. This is a very personal way to share the healing experience. It can be carried out on your own if the other person is not physically present, or if you can sit together and share the visualisation the healing can feel even more powerful. The Violet Flame Healing Temple is one retreat of Archangel Zadkiel and Holy Amethyst, who is his female counterpart or 'twin flame'. The Temple is in the etheric realms above Earth.

Visualisation:

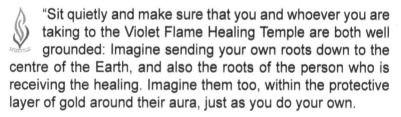 "Sit quietly and make sure that you and whoever you are taking to the Violet Flame Healing Temple are both well grounded: Imagine sending your own roots down to the centre of the Earth, and also the roots of the person who is receiving the healing. Imagine them too, within the protective layer of gold around their aura, just as you do your own.

Take a few deep breaths to relax and close your eyes. Imagine a staircase in front of you both, formed out of Amethyst crystal. Each step lights up as your feet touch it and the Amethyst glows. Your footsteps become lighter and lighter as you ascend the staircase until you feel as if you are floating up through the clouds. Imagine the sun shining on the tops of the clouds with a silvery white light (just as you would see from the window of a plane). You see columns rise, formed out of the silvery white clouds, creating the structure of a Temple. The Temple shines so brightly that you are not sure whether it is the sun reflecting on it, or the Temple itself is the source of the light. As the light turns to violet you can see that it is emitted from an open doorway. You and your companion enter theViolet Flame Healing Temple. Cool marble columns reflect the Violet Light yet the floor is soft and warm. As you walk down the entrance hall you see gold seats with deep purple velvet cushions on them, places to sit and relax as you bathe in the Violet Light. At the far end, the hall opens out to a circular room. Set into the floor at its centre is a round concave area lined with gold. Within that, the Violet Flame burns. Archangel Zadkiel and Holy Amethyst are there to greet you.

As you approach, the Flame grows and becomes higher than you both, it flickers and shines with all the colours of violet which reflect in the gold base and on the white marble walls. Archangel Zadkiel and Holy Amethyst gently guide you and your companion to stand in the Violet Flame. Turn to face your companion and take hold of their hands in yours. Look into their eyes and let them know that this is done with love. The Flame feels cool on your skin and you can breathe in the beautiful colours of light. You may see or sense darker patches within either of you dissolving away, transmuted by the Violet Flame which cleanses and burns away any negativity, fear or unresolved issues, healing you both throughout.

Once your energy and that of your companion is clear and pure, step out through the other side of the flame. You may feel a cloak or wrap placed around your shoulders by the Archangels, or you can just take the opportunity to sit and talk with the person you have taken there with you, whilst still bathed in the Violet Light of the Flame.

When you are ready, return your awareness to the present, and thank Archangel Zadkiel and Holy Amethyst for their assistance. Imagine seeing whoever you have taken to the Violet Flame Healing Temple as being healthy, happy and healed.

Instant healing

A quick healing exercise to send the Violet Flame:

"Sit quietly; ground and protect yourself. Send your root down to the iron core centre of the Earth. Build the Violet Flame at your heart chakra and expand it out to fill the golden layer of light that surrounds your aura. Focus your thoughts on whoever you wish to send the Violet Flame to; you may like to have their photograph in front of you or have something written down, or even a crystal mandala that you had previously set for them.

You can also ask for the assistance of any of the Violet Flame Guardians and Directors, such as: Kuan Yin for Mercy and Forgiveness, St. Germain and his Lady Portia to transmute and rebalance awkward situations, or the Elohim Arcturus and Victoria to inspire a positive attitude.

With your palms facing each other, breathe the Violet Flame into the gap between. When you can see, sense or feel a tangible energy there, like a ball of Violet Flame held between your hands, blow through them as you turn your palms outward with the intent that the Violet Flame goes to surround the person you have sent it to. See them in your mind's eye surrounded in Violet Light; it will be there for them to absorb, if that is their choice. Bring your hands back to your heart chakra, one overlaying the other as if returning the Violet Flame to your own heart. Do not forget to thank any of the Guardians or

Directors of the Violet Flame if you had asked for their help.

Decree:

If you are not visual you may find it easiest to sit quietly and repeat a decree in multiples of three or seven, such as:

"I bring to the Temple of Violet Light
'...................' who is in need of help tonight."

You may prefer to regularly repeat any mantra or affirmation, or write one down and keep it in your sacred space. For example:

" '...................' is constantly surrounded with
Violet Flame. All negativity is transmuted.
He/She is healthy and happy. "

If it is appropriate and you feel comfortable explaining the Violet Flame's healing aspect, you could ask others to join you in creating a decree, mantra or affirmation and agree to repeat it at the same time each day. Like prayers, the energy builds each time it is repeated. It is not necessary to be with the person you are sending the healing to, for example, if they are in hospital. If you have a poorly relative, this method can unite a family to help focus on a positive outcome for them. It also gives a sense of purpose at a time when many feel helpless. A Violet Flame decree, mantra or affirmation is suitable for any-one from any religious background.

Mandala:

Write down the person's name and condition, and create a crystal mandala with whichever Violet Flame crystals you feel are the most effective for them. Even a simple shape will be sufficient; remember it is the focus of your intent and the power of your thoughts that carry the Violet Flame energy to wherever or whoever needs it. This can be a long term healing method, leaving the mandala out anywhere suitable, but do not let it gather dust! As the healing progresses, you may intuitively change any of the crystals at any time if you feel others would be more helpful. You can also 'recharge' your crystal healing mandala at any time by focusing the Violet Flame on it. The crystals hold the energy of your intent.

Photograph:

You can also send distant healing to someone using a photograph of them. Use it as a focus for your intent, as it often helps to see who you are sending healing to. This is an excellent way to send healing to someone you do not know or have never met. Occasionally I am asked to send Violet Flame healing to someone else's friend or relative, and I ask for a photograph of them, even if it is sent digitally to my phone or computer.

If you have an actual printed photograph, hold it in your hands and take a few deep breaths. Ground yourself, connecting to the centre of the Earth and build the Violet Flame energy at your heart chakra. Feel it expanding through your body and out into your aura. Focus the energy as an intense Violet Light seeping through from your hands into the photograph. Hold the thought in your mind that the Violet Flame is surrounding the person or people in it. It is there for them if they choose to absorb it. You may imagine them as being well, smiling and laughing, with all concerns transmuted to positive health and happiness. Hold the focus for a moment or two longer and imagine telling them that this healing is sent with love.

Sometimes I only have a digital image sent and stored on my computer to work from, and cannot print it to use the above method. I 'edit' the image with a violet colour, copy it onto a blank page, and write around it any Violet Flame healing affirmations that are appropriate. For example:

"The Violet Flame transmutes all negativity to create positive health and happiness".

or:

"This person, '....................' is healed and healthy within the energy of the Violet Flame."

Depending on how creative you are with a computer, this can be great fun. Your thoughts, intent, the time and energy taken will send the Violet Flame to the person, people, animals or situation in the digital image.

Even lighting a violet candle for someone and asking the Violet Flame to transmute the energy of their injury or illness will help them.

For Reiki Practitioners who use the symbols to send distant healing, imagine creating a cloud of Violet Flame energy to place the symbols on, sending the combination of healing energy.

I keep a Violet Flame Healing List and regularly before going to sleep I ask the Archangels Zadkiel and Holy Amethyst to surround each person on my list with Violet Flame energy while they sleep. I do not set any intent as it is then absorbed or not according to the will of the individual. The energy is merely there for them if they want it.

Any of these can be repeated as often as you like – you can't overdose on Violet Flame!

Take it to the limit!

Planetary Healing

There are many places on Earth that have experienced negativity just within our lifetime. Wars, famine, earthquakes, pollution, human destruction and natural disasters have all taken their toll. Now think back through history; there are very few places that have never had any upset or disruption. Scars remain even from hundreds and thousands of years ago. Negativity creates more negativity, and fear remains where disasters have occurred.

All life on this planet reacts to its environment, including us. For example, it is said that birds still do not sing at Auschwitz; they are reacting to the negative energy of the place due to past events there. People still experience a shudder at the site of the twin towers in New York. It was described to me as, "it just feels wrong to laugh or be happy there." Maybe that is just respect for those who lost their lives, but would any of them want the sadness to continue? We tend to perpetuate it by our own actions and reactions. Those too, are slowly changing as the negativity is released. I believe that so much has already been achieved by those who have prayed or sent healing, and by those who have anchored the Violet Flame there.

What sort of world could we create by clearing the effect of past disasters or destruction on Earth? It does not matter how long ago such events occurred. The Violet Flame transmutes negative energy to positive energy throughout time. Any fear, horror, or despair can be safely released from the Earth within the Violet Flame; scars will begin to heal and Life will return to a state of balance and harmony.

If countries that are struggling with unrest or on the brink of war could be flooded with Violet Flame, then surely solutions would be much easier to find within that positive light? Imagine the Earth at peace, filled with Violet Light, radiating out into the Universe. How many of us, focusing our intent, would it take to create that? We cannot possibly know, but surely whatever each one of us does will make some difference!

Let's go global

Sending distant Violet Flame healing to the Earth can be as simple as placing a globe within your sacred space, in your violet coloured box, or within an amethyst cave, for example. If you look around toy shops, you may find juggling or bouncing balls patterned with the countries of Earth, or a postcard of Earth from outer space, or download an image from the internet; the effort you put in at this stage is already carrying the focus of your intent. If you want to send the Violet Flame to a specific country, any troops fighting abroad, or an area hit by disaster, then find something that represents that individual place to you.

If you sit and hold a chosen representation of a certain place or of the whole planet, it is easiest to expand the Violet Flame through you to surround and seep to the centre of the object you hold. There is a reservoir of Violet Flame at the Earth's core and over central Europe, so you may ask any of the Guardians of that energy, St. Germain for example, to release it to wherever you are sending your focus. For planetary healing you can also send your thoughts to the Ruler of the Violet Planet, Omri-Tas, and ask him to release spheres of Violet Flame to drop on whole areas of Earth. (Personally I see these rather like waterbombs, exploding on impact, spraying the Violet Light out over the landscape.)

Healing for Animals and Nature

Using the Violet Flame to help animals, in fact anything and everything in Nature, is wonderful. All creatures naturally respond to this vibrational frequency with greater ease than we humans do. Your pets will react to the change in your energy field as you start to work regularly with the Violet Flame.

Anchor the Violet Flame for all animals and creatures when you are out in the open countryside, in woods, fields and rivers. They instinctively know where there is a place with a special energy where they can heal or recharge their own energy levels. Set one in your garden and notice how birds and animals are drawn there; you may like to mark it out with a circle of stones much like a 'fairy ring'. This is great fun to do with children too, as they retain a link to their spiritual selves and higher realms and are untainted by the world of adulthood.

My granddaughter and I regularly visit the places where we have set by thought, visualisation and intent, a sacred space for the animals and creatures in a nearby wood. We created a circle of small stones, stood within it, facing each other holding hands and, in her words: 'thought pretty mauve, all sparkly and light going down through me and out of my feet into the circle'. Together we asked that the Guardians of the wood keep this place safe and keep the Violet Flame alight here for all the creatures. Then we stepped out of the circle.

We counted our steps back to a stile which we kept as our marker and we go back when we can to clear any fallen leaves and twigs, refreshing the Violet Flame anchored there. It was suggested to me that if we were to put sand around our Violet Flame circle we would be able to see the footprints of which animals had visited it. My granddaughter wanted us to climb a nearby tree and watch, but it would have taken a lot of Violet Flame for me to be nimble enough to get up there!

It is wonderful to imagine a great bubble of Violet Flame in the middle of every sea and ocean where all the whales, dolphins and sea creatures can cleanse, heal and re-energise, bathing in the light that you have set there for them. At every river and stream you cross, extend the Violet Flame that you carry out into the water to flow to all the fish, birds and creatures of our waterways.

Whichever way you choose to use the Violet Flame for any creatures who are dear to your heart, whether by direct healing, distant healing or anchoring it to a certain place for them, they will receive it as a blessing from you. Even keeping a photograph of them in your sacred space or altar, or creating a crystal mandala for them, will be appreciated and helpful to their wellbeing. Every aspect of nature gratefully receives this natural spiritual energy as Earth is, at heart, a Spiritual Planet.

Away with the Fairies, the Gnomes, the Mermaids and the Fire Dragons

For the Elementals

The Elementals are those unseen guardians of the elements of Earth, Air, Fire, and Water. They are known by many different names over the world, but are depicted in art and folklore just about everywhere. In England the Fairies are called Sylphs and guard the element of Air, the Mermaids are Undines guarding Water, and the Fire Dragons are called Salamanders naturally guarding the Fire element. The Gnomes guard the Earth element and seem to keep that name wherever you go. The elements of our Earth were the first aspects of this planet to settle and balance when it was still forming, so the Elementals were here long before any other life could evolve.

With all the pollution and damage to the Earth that mankind has wrought, it is even harder for these beings to maintain the balance. The Violet Flame is the best tool they have, too. If we can work together and further enhance the Violet Flame for them to use, the elements of the Earth, Air, Fire and Water can be healed back to a state of harmony and balance. Because they are part of nature and the natural elements of the Earth, they are happy sharing the places where we anchor the Violet Flame for the animals.

CHAPTER 9

Summary

Healing

● The Violet Flame can be used for healing on its own, or combined with any other healing method

● As with any healing, it must always be done with the permission of the recipient and the intent that it is for the Highest Good. Ask that the Violet Flame be received when they are at home and relaxed or asleep at night.

● Healing with the Violet Flame is not a "quick fix" or a "cure all" for every problem. Some health issues are part of life's experiences and the Violet Flame can help ease that process.

● Combining the Violet Flame with the chakra colours will transmute negativity which can block the natural flow of energy through the chakras.

● The Violet Flame can be sent to any person, animal, place, or situation, now, in the past or the future.

● Visualising taking someone with you to the Violet Flame Healing Temple is a very personal way to share the healing experience.

● A Violet Flame crystal healing mandala will hold the focus for healing to be sent continuously over a period of time.

● You can also send the Violet Flame as distant healing to someone using a photograph of them.

● You can't overdose on Violet Flame!

● All animals, creatures, and the Elementals react instinctively to the Violet Flame. Create an anchor for them when you are out in the open countryside, in woods, fields and rivers.

CHAPTER 10

PAST LIVES AND KARMA

Because violet is the highest vibration of visible light, reaching beyond it leads us into the realms of our higher selves and the path towards our own spiritual enlightenment. Working regularly with the Violet Flame helps us on that journey. The Flame itself is the impetus to carry us forward, to drive us higher, further into that Violet Ray of light. In this way our physical selves, our higher selves, our spirits and souls can be freed from their burdens. When this has been achieved, all aspects of our selves will be reunited.

To assist in achieving spiritual enlightenment, the Violet Flame can clear the past patterns and programming of our human existence. It releases us from restrictive ideas and misconceptions, allowing us the freedom to live the path we chose. By shedding the heavy load of negative emotions, healing the scars and wounds of our previous lifetimes, and learning from the issues and expectations we have, we achieve positive attributes such as wisdom, knowledge, compassion, understanding and love.

Karma is the word frequently used to describe the balance or imbalance of all our actions and intentions throughout our many lifetimes. Before we can reach the end of our physical incarnations and 'ascend' to the higher planes of existence, we need to have settled all these outstanding issues; any debts must be repaid and we must have learnt all that our Higher Selves or souls wanted to learn here on Earth. If we are discovering and learning about an issue like trust, for example, we will have several lives with this common theme, experiencing trust from all different aspects and perspectives: trusting too easily and being hurt or betrayed, betraying someone else's trust, unable to trust and so withdrawing from people, helping a child or partner dealing with this issue, and so forth. There is no limit as to how many lives in which this one matter can occur, as we strive to understand it totally. Each life usually has many such threads running through it.

It may seem daunting that all these must eventually balance out and our lessons be completed. But remember we are not limited by time, there is no deadline and we decide when we have completed each 'lesson' and understood each issue fully. It is one of the reasons for reincarnation. I'm sure that when we return to Spirit after each life, with an understanding of our experiences and what we have learnt, that there will always be a 'Yes, but... what about if...?' So we return here to find out a bit more, look with greater depth, understand a little more fully and achieve the wisdom we seek. As each issue is ticked off our list, so to speak, the Violet Flame will transmute any of the negative energy that we have acquired or absorbed during such lives. We do tend to learn the most from the hardest experiences and most difficult emotions.

I believe that as we leave and arrive on this Earth through the Violet Ray of Light, much of that negativity is automatically transmuted; however some is retained to have an effect on any future life to further enhance our understanding. It is that retained negativity that we can consciously transmute during each lifetime to assist the learning process with less pain, hurt and upset. It is worth mentioning too, that as we are all interconnected, each one of us affects others we come into contact with and they affect our lives. Many situations balance out in time, not always through our own doing; sometimes our karmic debts are interlocked with another person, and as that person settles their issues, then ours are automatically cleared.

So how can we distinguish between what is for us to clear and what will automatically clear by the actions of others or be transmuted on our return to Spirit? Our own intuition may give the answer to this question. If this does not provide clarity, we can ask any of the Lords of Karma to assist us by accessing our Akashic Records.

We can also ask that they provide an opportunity for us to settle a matter by either bumping into or hearing from someone that we may need closure with. It is wonderful when that happens out of the blue and we know that our request has been heard and answered!

Where did that come from?

Recognising skills, gifts and talents

Throughout many lifetimes you accumulate positive and negative experiences that help you to learn and grow. The skills, gifts and talents from previous lifetimes, your core personality, the deepest part of your self and identity are all positive attributes that you carry forward with you on your spiritual journey. It is widely recognised that some of your gifts and talents are inherited from your parents, but what if you chose precisely those parents for the opportunity to enhance certain positive attributes that you have already acquired in a previous life?

I believe that in planning our reincarnation we do choose and pre-agree the parents and family we will return amongst. In knowing several of my own past lives, I can see my core personality; the issues I have now are ones that I can trace back though my soul's history. This includes a thread of creativity, skills that I have learnt many times over, my scientific interests and desire to understand the Universe, even my spiritual and psychic nature. All these traits are also evident in my family, so I have no doubt that this is by design and not accident. Through the Violet Flame and the Violet Light of the spiritual realms, I have been able to see my own journey so much more clearly. I can now appreciate my role in my present family within the context of our other shared lifetimes. Being able to see from a wider perspective, I came to understand our connections with each other and with the places we have lived, the times we have lived in and the effects we have had on each other, even the reasons for my sister's shortened life this time.

Over time, I gradually pieced together my understanding of our different relationships with each other. On each occasion I built up the Violet Flame energy within me from the spark of it at my heart and extended it to encompass my whole family and surroundings and then expanded that back through time.

For example, my father this time had been my brother in a life lived as Algonquin Indians, my sister had been my mentor in a life when I struggled as an aspiring playwright in Ancient Greece; in fact we had connected many times, not always as family, not all in the same time and sometimes only for a brief part of a lifetime. These glimpses of the connections we have previously made were as complex as a spider's web and I am still occasionally exploring other threads as my 'family' continues to grow, not only with children and grandchildren but also relationships that naturally come to include other people. We tend to reincarnate with members of our 'soul group' as these are the souls we can have pre-agreements with to share experiences and learn from each other.

By looking at my family through the Violet Light, I could appreciate which various talents I had genetically inherited from them and which I had built up in previous lifetimes. Added to these were the skills I learned from individual family members. In discovering that we shared some of the same skills and talents, I was able to work alongside my sister and take over from her when she passed away, as I know we had pre-agreed.

This may sound a bit clinical and analytical but in writing down and looking at my findings, all our strengths and weaknesses, I could feel a much closer bond that I could see went far beyond this one lifetime. I could then enhance within the Violet Flame any of those attributes that I wished to develop, removing any obstacles and transmuting any doubts about my abilities. Luckily for all those around me, singing was not on the list!

I kept my list with a piece of amethyst in my sacred space and drew a violet and purple mandala for my family, frequently imagining both items being engulfed in Violet Light.

I.O.U.

Karmic debts - to others

It has long been understood that we incur energy debts to each other throughout our many encounters and incarnations. Our interactions are complex as we willingly taking on roles to support or help others in their learning and they do the same for us. We learn the most from each other, from sharing experiences and interacting in many ways and types of relationships. Our paths may cross and cross back over again many times, creating a web so intricate that it becomes hard to know who owes what and to whom.

The best we can do is to hold the intent that all our karma is balanced this lifetime. That means that opportunities arise for us to fulfil our promises to each other and settle our debts. We can project our intent forward in time to help avoid and minimise any further karmic debt. Holding this thought within the Violet Flame will intensify its power.

I knew of a couple who were absolutely devoted to each other and were highly evolved souls, very aware of their previous lives together. They joyfully admitted that in one life she had killed him and another time he had killed her. They had explored many different lifetimes where their paths had crossed: in opposing armies in battle, as parent and child, as a bully and victim, as teacher and pupil, releasing their karma always within the Violet Flame. This time they were united; they worked, taught and lived together in a state of complete acceptance and unconditional love, which they chose to maintain, creating no more issues between them so that they could bring to a close their physical lives on Earth together. This is perhaps an extreme example, as I have never known anyone else quite like them, but one that I would choose to follow!

I.0.Me

Karmic debts - to our own soul/Higher Self

I once attended a talk given by a wonderful Tibetan Lama who was discussing the issue of karma. He told us that the promises and debts we exchange with other souls here in life are not considered true karma in their belief, but that karma is the agreement we have with our soul. We owe it to our soul, he said, to experience life to the fullest and to learn as many lessons as we can during our time here. That is real karma. When we simply repeat the way we react to situations from past experience, we are not learning. He explained that although it is within our human nature to respond in the same way each time we are in similar circumstances, we should try to react differently each time. It is a bit like 'Groundhog Day' (an American film and expression for repeating something over and over until you get it right). If we consciously change the way we react to repeated situations in our lives, then we are experiencing different aspects of it each time and that fulfils our agreement with our soul or Higher Self. Ultimately, we get it right!

That made me realise that all my preconceived ideas about karma needed to be re-examined. As is my practice, I view things like this within the Violet Flame where I find that any distortion of facts, untruths and even exaggerations just disappear, leaving only the truth behind. I found my existing perception of karma was still true for me, but felt the concept from the Tibetan Lama to be accurate and appropriate as well. As we expand our awareness and our connection to our Higher Selves, we need to also take these agreements with our soul into consideration. It is indeed, karma.

> *"What is done... is done"*
> – William Shakespeare (Macbeth)

Karma from previous lifetimes

If you are aware of karma from a past life, either through regression, or flashbacks, or perhaps a sixth sense or intuitive feeling, you may visualise going back to that life to bring about a peaceful solution. This will have a 'ripple effect' through time to alleviate any of the difficulties you may be experiencing because of it. Call for Archangel Michael to cut any cords and ties that may be holding you back, still connecting you to that lifetime and causing an inability to move on in this one. It is rather good to see it settled, and to feel the energy coming through to you in this lifetime as being free and clear.

Begin by ensuring you are grounded well and have connected to the heart or core of the Earth; with a few deep breaths build the Violet Flame within you, filling your entire body and aura. Ask your own Guides, one of the Lords of Karma or Archangel Michael to help you visualise the previous life's experience that you feel has left some karmic imbalance and replay it in your mind as if you are there. If the situation is too hurtful to take your mind back to, imagine watching it on a cinema screen so that you are a little more detached, or ask your Guides to explain it to you so that you know the facts without the emotion involved, until you are ready to face it yourself. Spread the Violet Flame out to encompass all concerned, the situation and surroundings. See or sense as many details as you can; colours, smells and sounds all make the experience more real and the 'ripple effect' stronger. Set the intent that the effects of any unbalanced karma will be neutralised, settling the matter for the Highest Good of all.

Once all negative energy has turned to positive thoughts and feelings, resolving the matter, bring your awareness back to yourself by focusing on your breathing. Thank those you've asked for help. Have a drink of water. Be prepared to cry; there is sometimes a real physical reaction to 'letting go' of a past situation. If it has been an emotional experience and leaves you feeling unsettled, refocus on your grounding roots to help you regain some stability and composure.

You can continue to imagine that any other person involved is surrounded constantly with the Violet Flame energy. Over time, they will respond to it without knowing why.

You can repeat this as often as you like, for you may experience different aspects each time until you feel the matter is completely resolved. Karma often builds up in layers, like an onion, that need to be peeled off bit by bit until you get to the very core of the potentially painful experience. You can include asking Archangel Zadkiel and Holy Amethyst to help you forgive, Lady Portia for justice (fairness and balance – not revenge!) and St. Germain for freedom from painful memories.

Have we met? I'm sure I know you

Recognition of a previous connection

Sometimes when meeting someone new, they feel so familiar that we are sure we have known them before. It is often an expression in their eyes that we recognise. This can happen at any time and in any situation, and may feel comfortable or not. When we feel an instant aversion to someone we meet, it is often due to a previous lifetime when we have 'crossed swords' with them, sometimes quite literally! Likewise we are drawn to people we have loved before even if we have chosen not to be together romantically this time. In these circumstances it is always helpful to explore any outstanding karmic debts or agreements with them.

> Having met a new man and feeling a sense of recognition, I suspected a karmic situation with him. Later I sat quietly and asked Kuan Yin, as one of the Lords of Karma, to show me the connection we had made previously and if it needed settling in order to bring balance to the relationship this time. I became less and less aware of my physical body as my consciousness went back to the time of the Spanish inquisition and my faith was in conflict to the orthodox Catholic Church. I felt as if I was walking down damp, cold tunnels leading to castle dungeons. The atmosphere of complete calm was a surprise in this awful place and I looked through a heavy iron barred door into one of the cells. I saw a young woman praying and immediately I knew that this was me. I took a deep breath in and let it out as a long sigh, as I entered the cell with her, knowing this entire lifetime in a second.

> I felt Kuan Yin in there with me, telling me that the jailer I would see was the man I had currently met in this lifetime. I asked her if he was a good man then, and she told me that his actions due to his position were not felt in his heart and he struggled with that conflict.

I listened to the shutting of another gate and heavy footsteps approaching. I prayed in the silence. They key went into the lock and turned almost in slow motion. I heard the scrape on the stone floor of the heavy metal gate opening and looked up to see the face of my jailer. There was something familiar in his eyes but the flickering light or a burning torch behind him gave me only a momentary image. I understood what Kuan Yin had meant. For this overpowering man, the requirements of his duty were not reflected in his heart. My own heart seemed to skip a beat as I withdrew.

My thoughts and awareness returned to my physical body. I sat with my eyes still closed and asked Kuan Yin how that lifetime had ended. She replied that I had been hanged as a heretic and the last thing I had seen were my jailer's eyes and the sorrow reflected in them. That explained why there seemed to be unfinished karma between us. It had been quite a dramatic glimpse into my past, but I could at least understand now why I had been so unsettled by his eyes when I first met him.

I then boosted the Violet Flame within me, filling my aura, and let my imagination return me to the scene I had witnessed in my meditation. I extended the Violet Flame energy out to fill the cell in the dungeon, seeping through to the core of my previous self kneeling there alone and praying. I expanded it, reaching out to all the other cells and to all the jailers, asking that Archangel Zadkiel radiate mercy and forgiveness in the Violet Flame to all those present at that time, spreading it further out to the gallows, executioner and all the experiences I had suffered in that lifetime and to all those involved.

I repeated this several times over the weeks as I began the new relationship. He was very protective of me this time, always trying to understand my point of view, and allowed me the space to enjoy my spiritual freedom. For my part I was able to give him the reassurance that I understood him, and accepted him for how he was and what he did.

With the Violet Flame and the help of the Lords of Karma, I have settled many karmic issues and had 'closure' on several very painful experiences this lifetime, with the very important attributes of mercy and forgiveness that the Violet Flame carries.

> *"Scars have the strange power to remind us that our past is real."*
>
> – Cormac McCarthy

Old wounds and scars

Physical injuries and scars in this lifetime last far beyond the accident or mishap that caused them. Emotional wounds frequently take even longer to heal. 'Scars' of both physical accidents and emotional upsets experienced in other lifetimes can often intrude into this life. People report conditions that defy medical diagnosis or treatment, for example, experiencing pain with no known cause. These unclassified problems can be considerably helped and often cleared completely with the healing of the Violet Flame. Sometimes it is just a matter of understanding and 'letting go' of the past experience. Sometimes they act as a reminder of previous battle scars and a warrior-like strength that can assist us in this lifetime. Birth marks are also sometimes thought to be scars received in a previous life and can simply be a reminder that we have lived before! The Violet Flame will transmute any negative energy that may have caused them to become a problem in this lifetime.

When I was studying crystal healing and practising on one of my fellow students, I felt an anomaly in his energy field over his right shoulder. I checked with my crystal pendulum dowser, as we had been taught to do, and the crystal reacted strongly to the change in energy at that spot. It felt as if something was sticking out of him when I passed my hand or the crystal over his shoulder. The teacher told me to check the back of his shoulder to see if something had passed all the way through, and when I did so I had the image in my mind of an arrow.

In that instant I could see him riding on a horse through a forest, travelling from a nearby monastery. I was sitting above in a tree next to a man with a bow and arrow ready to fire. It was a time of religious troubles, monastic dissolution, and widespread uncertainty. There were small bands of rebels fighting for freedom. I recognised the rider below as a good man, but my companion loosed his arrow just as I put my hand on his arm to stop him. I was a fraction of a second too late!

The arrow had manifested in this lifetime at precisely the moment when I was able to balance that karmic debt between us. I removed the energy of the arrow and healed the past injury with the Violet Flame. I learnt that day how to deal with such incidents and was amazed at the power of the Violet Flame to heal through time. It had been some 470 years since the incident. Richard's shoulder was healing in the present because the Violet Flame had gone back in time to the moment he was shot, transmuting the negative energy of the injury. We also had the opportunity to forgive the mistake and make amends for it.

Afterwards Richard said that he had always had a problem with that shoulder and it clicked every time he raised his arm or went swimming. Not any more!

During years of healing clients since then, I have discovered an assortment of wounds, scars, and even objects that are clearly not from this time. Nevertheless they do relate to the individual's life in a way that causes pain or difficulty without any known cause. Some of the energetic anomalies have been weapons, including arrows, spears, and shrapnel, that I can see and feel in a psychic sense not in a physical sense. These show up out of the blue when they are ready to be cleared and for the most part manifest when some karmic issue from previous life is being worked through.

Once I have removed any item found and transmuted its energy in the Violet Flame, I then psychically search for the original action or event that has been causing the disturbance in the present. Upon sending the Violet Flame to that point in time, the pain or difficulty usually lessens or disappears.

Rosie, a client, friend and Reiki student of mine over many years, complained on one visit of feeling trapped. We both assumed it was due to having two young children and not much free time to herself. I saw the sudden manifestation of the energy of barbed wire wrapped around her legs. As she described how she was feeling unable to move forward with her own healing practice, I saw the barbed wire tighten until it was digging into her flesh. She went absolutely white when I told her what I could psychically see. She confided that she had always had an unexplained fear of barbed wire in this lifetime.

I gently removed the energy and healed her legs with both Violet Flame and Reiki (as they work so well together). I then directed the Violet Flame back to an incident I could see in another life that had caused her to become ensnared in barbed wire and the terror she had felt at not being able to flee from the approaching enemy. We worked together to transmute that fear from her life then and now.

As part of her Reiki training, Rosie was practising self-healing, giving herself daily Reiki treatments. Following the session where we cleared the barbed wire, she continued to incorporate the Violet Flame with her Reiki. She managed to clear all the after effects of her experience and no longer felt trapped. She has since taken her Reiki Practitioner level and is growing in awareness and healing abilities.

So it is written...

The Akashic Records

If you are struggling with an issue in this lifetime that you cannot trace back to your childhood or make any sense of and so feel it may have come from another lifetime, you may finds its source in your Akashic Records. These are a record of all your thoughts, intentions and actions from all your past incarnations on your soul's journey, written by your Higher Self in absolute truth and honesty. Your Akashic Records are for your use only, as they contain personal and private information.

Whether or not you are aware of any previous incarnation, you can ask any one of the Lords of Karma to accompany you. Kuan Yin and Lady Portia are among the Lords of Karma who are particularly associated with the Violet Flame and can assist you in its use to transmute karmic energy. They represent the qualities of Mercy, Forgiveness, and Justice, all of which are essential to settling these matters. They will add to your confidence and clarity in understanding the situations which may have led to an imbalance. They will also ensure that the Violet Flame will balance only karma that is ready to be settled and is for the Highest Good.

It was Lady Portia who accompanied me in meditation to see my own Akashic records. She is the twin flame of St. Germain who brought knowledge of the Violet Flame back into the consciousness of mankind early in the twentieth century. She is often depicted carrying the scales of justice and the sword of truth. She helps us to balance our karmic debts without judgement or emotional desire for revenge. With her scales we can weigh up the facts, the emotions and the outcome, seeing the whole issue as part of our soul's journey and ensuring that it does indeed balance.

The easiest way to access your records is through meditation.

 As you ground yourself in preparation, feel the energy of the Violet Flame building up from your heart chakra to extend throughout your physical body and your aura. At this stage, you can ask for assistance from one of the Karmic Lords.

Your may visualise your Akashic Records as a huge old book in some ancient library. Imagine being there and notice your surroundings. A book will have been left out for you; it may be large, old and leather bound. Feel the texture of its cover and connect with this book as it contains all your personal records. Ask to be shown any situation or issue with an outstanding karmic debt. The pages of the book may flip over and fall open at a certain page or several pages, or you may open it yourself and intuitively know which page you need to see. You can ask to be shown the significance of what you see and read and how that relates to your present life. Expand the Violet Flame energy from your own aura to encompass the book, seeping through to its core. Watch Violet Flames burning off any negative energy or unsettled situations until the light surrounding the records is clear. You may see a gold line has been drawn across the page denoting the matter is settled, or the book simply closes. If one of the Karmic Lords has been assisting you, they will take care of your Akashic Records until you may wish to access them again. Give them your thanks as you gently bring your awareness back to the present.

Akashic Records have been experienced by some as a film on a screen, or even a computer programme. If this image comes to your mind when focusing on the Violet Flame to balance

Karma, that is fine. You can sit and watch a film of your lives and find the screen may 'freeze' at a certain point. Expand the Violet Flame out from your aura to encompass every part of the screen or section of the film that is relevant to the karmic issue. When the negativity has been transmuted, the film ends. If other people appear in your 'film', the Violet Flame will carry the attributes of Mercy, Forgiveness, and Justice to them wherever they are at present.

When you ask for assistance, you will see your Akashic Records represented in whichever way is appropriate and easiest for you to understand. Even in meditation, some people like to read a book; others would prefer to watch the film!

If you find it difficult to access your Akashic Records at first, you may find it helps to be talked through the process. This should only be done with someone you completely trust. There are some spiritual healers or teachers who have practice in accessing these records. I would advise against anyone who offers to settle these matters on your behalf, as it is your journey, your lessons to understand and your personal records. It would be like giving someone else your diary to read when you cannot remember quite what you have written!

> *"You may forget your past,*
> *but your past does not forget you"*
> – Author unknown

Settling unknown karma

If you are not visual or find meditation daunting, you may use any other method you choose. You might feel more comfortable writing a letter to Kuan Yin, Lady Portia or even your own Higher Self. Ask that any unbalanced karma which is ready to be settled be infused with the Violet Flame. Write down that you forgive yourself and all others involved, whether the karmic situations are in your conscious memory or not. Finally, ask that a gold line be drawn under these matters. Most importantly write from your heart and in your own words. This is not a technical exercise, it is a letter to those Higher Beings, including yourself, who love and watch over you unconditionally. If there is any remaining karma which you have not fully understood and learnt from, it cannot be cleared at this present time. Ask for an opportunity to arise whereby you can learn the same lesson and settle the karma when appropriate.

If you are aware of any unsettled karma from a previous lifetime, you may wish to focus on that, particularly if it involves another person who you know in this lifetime too. You can draw the infinity symbol (Lemniscate) in violet and write your name in one loop and the name of the other person in the other loop. If you can, include any details or the issue you are struggling with. Trace the symbol over and over with the pen, with a crystal such as Sugilite or Amethyst, or with your finger, visualising the Violet Flame flowing along and connecting the two sides, the two people or situations, and uniting them in balance and harmony. Ask one of the Lords of Karma to balance all outstanding issues. As the symbol is one of infinite time, a continuous loop, it works very well with matters that are beyond this life's time.

Keep the Violet Flame flowing through and around your written requests, letters or drawings, surrounding them in Violet Light. You can place them on your altar or sacred space with any of the Violet Flame crystals, or use a violet coloured ribbon to tie them with a picture of Kuan Yin or Lady Portia. You may like to focus on them every week or every month, holding them together and asking that the Violet Flame continues to burn off any negative karmic energy. You can keep them as long as you feel necessary then burn them in the flame of a violet candle.

You can either use decrees, mantras or an affirmation, repeated daily in multiples of three or seven.

For example:

 "The Violet Flame balances and settles my karmic debts with unconditional love for the Highest Good of all."

Following any work to settle or balance karma, be prepared for an increase in synchronicity. For example: bumping into someone you were just thinking of, meeting new people in unexpected places and finding that you share interests, feeling unduly emotional over a particular news items or being drawn to a magazine article that you would not normally pick up and read. These are often indications of the 'ripple effect' through time of having settled some karma that you may not have been consciously aware of.

Did I do that?

Accepting that we are not always 'the good guy'

We have all done things in our previous lives which we would not be proud of this time. We have to remember that in order to experience fully a situation, issue or emotion, we need to be on the giving and receiving end as well as live the part of observer, dealing with it through another's perception. We do this by helping someone, often our child or partner who is working through the same things we have already experienced and so we incarnate with them to help them through it, so that we also may gain a greater understanding. We should also take into consideration the cultural times of any previous lives where we have been 'the baddie'. Throughout history we have seen barbaric times and mankind continues to behave atrociously to one another in certain situations, particularly war. These actions have to be seen in the context of the time.

If you have an experience or are told of a previous life when you may have acted in such a way that causes you distress, please remember that this is just one part of your learning process and that no single life is entirely 'good' or entirely 'bad', that ultimately all your lives are lived in balance. To achieve that balance you experience the extremes.

I have found the best way to deal with these pieces of the jigsaw that is our whole journey, is to write them down and burn them in the flame of a violet candle. I ask the Karmic Lords to release the burden from my heart, mind and soul. I have done this several times until the knowledge no longer upsets me. We are not here, alive on this Earth, to get it right every time. We have all made mistakes, experienced the 'lows' as well as the 'highs' in order to learn. I hold the desire to transmute these lifetimes and the pain I may have caused others, I have the intent to learn from them, and the Violet Flame does the rest.

"We learn from failure, not from success!"
                              – Bram Stoker (Dracula)

This life's karma

We all know of someone who got their 'just desserts' eventually. Occasionally we read in the paper of a person who had behaved really badly, only to have the same thing happen to them by someone else. We can't help feeling a little smug can we? There is a certain satisfaction in seeing that karmic debt repaid! On some level, we all recognise that this is fair, just and necessary. We hope that they learnt their lesson, otherwise the karma will continue until they do.

Situations occur throughout our present lives that are left unfinished. The times we say:
'I wish I'd said this... or that'
'If only we hadn't parted on such bad terms', and even:
'I owe you a favour'. These are all little snippets of karma that

we have the chance to settle regularly, by focusing daily on the Violet Flame.

I usually ask for the opportunity to settle any of these outstanding little debts on a weekly basis, and so often find that within a few days I bump into or hear from someone that I need to settle something with. Occasionally I become aware of a much bigger issue or a regret that I may have carried for a long time, or I hear from a third party that someone holds a grudge or has been wishing to settle some issue of their own which involved me. I do write these down and specifically use the Violet Flame to clear anything that is blocking their settlement. It does not usually take long before we have the chance to resolve things.

You cannot erase the past, you cannot even change it, but sometimes life offers you the opportunity to put right any injustice or imbalance. It is helpful to know what you want closure for, and what you want to rebalance. For example: friends you have lost contact with, but maybe feel you still owe them a debt – something you were never able to repay them, a debt of kindness, an actual monetary debt, or simply something you wished you had said. It may be that you had a disagreement, or fell out with them, and with hindsight wish you had been able to make up again. By using The Violet Flame you can start a pathway to reconciliation; ask that you meet up again or find them on a social networking website for example. Once you have taken the initiative, and set the intent for a karmic debt to be repaid, the Violet Flame will enhance the process to a successful conclusion.

It wasn't me!

Releasing guilt

This is a tricky one because we all like to forget the things we have done that we have not owned up to! We must search our own consciences for anything that we know we really should have taken responsibility for – but did not. We can use the Violet Flame to smooth out any effects resulting from our not owning up, such as someone else getting the blame. There's a karmic debt! Usually these small slips are totally harmless and do not adversely affect another person but they remain in our conscience and still need to be cleared. The Violet Flame is an easy and very private way of doing so, unless we really are driven to 'owning up'.

Valerie was in her seventies and I had known her for many years as a totally honest lady with high morals and critical judgement. It came as a huge shock when one day she admitted to me that years previously she had scratched and dented her husband's car by reversing into a post that she had not seen. She then told him it had been damaged in a car park while she had been shopping and she did not see who the culprit was! It seemed so out of character that I couldn't help my surprise showing on my face. She said she had always carried the guilt that her husband had paid for the repair rather than lose his no-claims bonus on the insurance. She really thought there was no point in telling him now as he was showing signs of dementia and it would trouble him, so she asked me if the Violet Flame could release her guilt.

I encouraged her to talk through the accident, describing the location, where she was reversing and so forth. She could even remember what she had been wearing, so this must have replayed in her mind many, many times. She easily recalled the sound of the car hitting the post, her pulling forward a little and putting on the handbrake, getting out to see the damage and her feelings as she sat and wondered what to do. They did not have much money at that time in their lives and she thought that her husband could claim on their insurance if she told him it was an accident caused by someone untraceable. Having never claimed before she thought it was the best solution.

As it was the subsequent lie to her husband that she felt guilty about rather than the accident itself, that is what we focused on. I asked her where she felt the guilt was now: within her somewhere, or had she placed it elsewhere externally? Valerie replied that it was both. She felt a knot at the pit of her stomach and recognised that as the guilt, but she had also written down her confession and hidden it in a box in their loft. She always thought that if she were to die first then he would find it and that would be her way of saying sorry, but now there was a chance that she would outlive him she felt she had to deal with it on her own. I felt quite honoured that she had shared this secret burden with me and gratitude that she is now allowing me to share it with you. Although to many this may not be a big issue, it certainly was to this honest, upright lady.

Her confession in the loft was easily found and quite cere-moniously burned in the flame of a violet candle. She liked the idea of making a little speech as we held the paper in long tweezers over the flame, watching it burn, and the rising smoke taking her guilt with it. She said that alone eased the knot in her stomach, but she continued to focus the Violet Flame there until that too had gone.

During one easy, lucid time with her husband Bill, she actually told him all about it. He laughed and said he'd guessed that was the case all along!

Missed opportunity?

How long does karma last?

Sometimes the other person is unwilling to let go of anger or betrayal that has gathered over a long period of time and this can be frustrating for the person who is ready to move on. When karmic situations occur between two people whose lives are closely entwined, like partners, business partners and family members, it is very hard to distinguish when the karma is settled. If there has been no closure to a disagreement or falling out, then it is always worthwhile to seek that for your own peace of mind, regardless as to whether it is karma or not.

I add these people and situations to my Violet Flame healing list and regularly send that out with my thoughts, so that whenever they are ready the energy is there to create the opportunity.

That opportunity came for one pair of ex-business partners who happened to be in the same place at the same time, years after their partnership had broken down. One of the ex-partners, Jack, had asked for the opportunity to settle the issue between them, as they had previously had a good friendship, and he no longer wanted the bad feelings between them. Personality clashes had led to the other partner pulling out of the business they had started together, leaving Jack to run it alone and he built the business up. However, it had since closed for other reasons and Jack felt it was time to have closure on their partnership and friendship issues.

He set that intent and asked for an opportunity to arise. Some time later, in a large out-of-town department store, they happened to be at the same counter at the same time! Sadly, the other party was clearly not ready to let go of his resentment over the business, saw but ignored Jack and turned away. Jack was naturally disappointed and asked me if this missed opportunity led to even more karma building up between them. I believe that as it was still the same issue, the karma continues until the grievance or debt is settled, closure and forgiveness are achieved. It will simply run on, but the intent has been activated by Jack. I talked him through their accidental meeting, visualising the Violet Flame all around them both, and we worked together to create another such opportunity so that when the time is right for the other partner, the energy will be there to resolve matters. He continues to send his thoughts out for a happy conclusion and holds the intent with a crystal mandala.

'I'm going to miss you!'

No karma to settle

Just occasionally we have a bond with someone else which could easily be misconstrued as a karmic debt or karmic agreement. It is worthwhile looking at these through the Violet Flame to understand them better. As we reincarnate with other members of our soul group, we can and do offer unconditional support to each other without any payback or balance required. This love for each other transcends any one lifetime and when it is recognised as such, our lives are so much richer and fuller for the acknowledgement of it.

Many years ago I moved house, leaving the town where I had my children and one very close friend who I knew I would miss terribly. She was struggling with things in her life at the time and I felt guilty leaving her, as she had helped and supported me through some really tough times of my own. However it was unavoidable, I had to go. We were both aware of having known each other before and belonging to the same soul group; I always felt very close to her children too. So clearly there were bonds and ties here that went far beyond this lifetime. I still felt an outstanding karmic debt though, as I simply had not been there to help her through her challenges as she had been for me.

All I could do was send love, healing and the Violet Flame to her along with lengthy telephone calls which did help to allay my worry and concern for her, and my own feelings of missing her. The guilt I felt was something I had to deal with separately and first I needed to understand what the karmic debts were. As I looked through some of the many photos of us all together and focused my attention on the Violet Flame for an overview, transmuting the blockages of time and distance, I saw that we had chosen to be here this time purely for mutual support, that all previous karma had been settled long ago. That made me feel even worse! When I had needed her she was with me every day; but where was I when she needed me? Over a hundred miles away. Even though I knew it would not break our friendship, her sadness, frustration and feelings of being let down must have been immense. I wanted to honour our pre-agreed promise of mutual support and with the Violet Flame I could. Through many of its applications I hold the intent of keeping that promise to our friendship, sending distant healing, taking her to the Violet Flame Temple, sending protection to her children and more recently teaching her daughter the power of the Violet Flame. For me everything is in balance because that energy is given unconditionally between two very good friends; there is no karma to settle, it is choice.

No more karma, please!

Creating karmic debts to settle in the future

We cannot help creating these situations daily just by our interaction with each other, but be conscious of instigating any major or lasting imbalances with others. At the end of every day or even at the end of the week, think back and see if there are any loose ends that need tying. Wrap them visually in the light of the Violet Flame, or write them down with a mantra or leave a crystal with them – set the intent that these matters will be brought together or completed.

Try to experience life and all its opportunities newly each day. It is hard not to repeat patterns but by thinking of the karmic agreements you have with your Higher Self or your soul, you can set your intent to respond differently each time. The power of your own thoughts and regular use of the Violet Flame will lessen the effects of karma in your life now and in the future.

By incorporating the Violet Flame into your regular routine, either by visualisation, repeating a mantra, or simply setting your intent to continually transform any negative energy within the Violet Light, karma will more often be settled as it happens. For example, I have a friend who weekly repeats three times the following affirmation:
"I clear and settle my karmic debts to myself and all others within the Violet Flame."
She keeps it written down on her sacred space and reads it aloud every Saturday morning – that is dedication for you!

Remember you cannot change what has already happened, only the energy of it, and reactions to it; it is the negative emotions which you can change. This has an effect like dropping a pebble in a pool, creating ripples outwards, so that any lessons can be understood. Forgiveness, justice and balance can be restored. When holding the Violet Flame within you and using the energy of it with your heart and mind, these changes can be instant. How wonderful to live a life with no debts!

World payback?

Karmic debts between Man and Earth

We cannot say when mankind started to misuse this planet and its resources, or when the Earth started to fight back. But over thousands of years karma has been building between us. We are now realising that mankind is part of Earth and not separate from it. We want to live in harmony with nature and settle all the imbalance of the past. This is our ongoing project for possibly the next millennium, but I believe we can all make a difference, however small, that will help release this huge karmic debt and edge us closer to achieving a life in harmony with our world.

I spent a thought provoking time one afternoon meditating with Master Rakoczy, also known as The Great Divine Director, and another one of the Lords of Karma. He presides over all incarnations of mankind; he holds the 'blueprints' of civilisations that have risen and fallen on this planet. I asked him about Earth's karma: are we as individuals responsible for all mankind's debts? He said:

"No one individual can take on that debt! It is a matter for the group or collective consciousness of mankind to realise the effect it has on this Earth, and to redress the balance over a far longer period than any one lifetime would allow. It is something that mankind has been working toward for a very long time, and slowly karma is being repaid and balanced. All the troubles on the planet and all the upset rising to the surface through human actions and Earth's actions, are in order to be cleared. The intent and the will are there; it holds true with enough souls presently incarnate on Earth for there to be a great karmic settlement. But it is a long process and not complete yet!"

If you feel drawn to include some of this in the settlement of your own karmic debts, then do not be daunted by the enormity of it! There is no Earth Bank Manager adding interest or sending you statements. Bit by bit we can achieve far more together than any one person alone, and because the restrictions of time are not relevant, your input can be done at any time to suit you. For example, on those occasions when you see or hear that it is 'World Peace Day', do join in with your thoughts, intent, and the Violet Flame. That focused intent was described to me by a friend as creating a laser-like Light that cuts through the grey and black cloud of interference. I found that rather hopeful!

We understand that healing starts within and we accept a degree of responsibility for our own health and wellbeing. We are learning to extend that same care and duty to our entire planet. We cannot go back and change what has been done, but we can at last look to the future with a sense of responsibility. We have the desire and the will to make a difference. We also have the Violet Flame to create the change. If we see or read of atrocities or disasters in the news, we can now choose to send the Violet Flame to ease the suffering; we are no longer helpless.

To balance karma for the planet, ask Archangel Zadkiel's Violet Flame Angels to spread their wings over Earth. Ask Omri-Tas, the ruler of the Violet Planet, to release spheres of Violet Flame to drop on areas of Earth where there is suffering, poverty, pollution or corruption. Violet Flame spheres can cover vast areas; dropping like water-bombs they explode on impact spraying their Violet Flame energy in all directions. Omri-Tas is always willing to help us in this way to clear our world of negative karma, transmuting the dis-ease caused by mankind, the weather, or the Earth itself.

With many of us working together and with the assistance of the Guardians and Directors of the Violet Flame, we can achieve a world of peace and harmony.

CHAPTER 10

Summary

Past lives and karma

◆ The Violet Flame helps you to identify and understand any skills, talents, and traits which have been acquired through experiences in previous lifetimes.

◆ You can settle karmic debts with the Violet Flame, whether they are to others or to your own soul/Higher Self.

◆ Recognition of another's soul can indicate a past life connection and sometimes this will be in order to settle some previous imbalance or debt. The Violet Flame will transmute any negativity that remains, so that the connection can be enjoyed.

◆ Unexplained wounds and scars can become apparent in this lifetime when balancing karmic issues. The Violet Flame will heal them.

◆ Your Akashic Records will show any matters which are unbalanced or unfinished. These can be settled within the Violet Flame so that you are not held back on your soul's journey.

◆ You do not have to be aware of any karmic debts in order to settle them with the Violet Flame. You can ask that opportunities arise in this lifetime to balance anything outstanding.

◆ The Violet Flame will help you to come to terms with having behaved badly. We are not always the 'good guys'.

◆ Closure on any outstanding issue within this lifetime can be achieved through working with the Violet Flame.

◆ The Violet Flame makes it easier to take responsibility for your actions by alleviating the worry of a bad reaction to your 'owning up'.

◆ Living your life in the Violet Flame lessens the chance of creating any new karmic situations, imbalances, or debts.

◆ The karmic debt between mankind and our planet Earth is, and remains, ongoing. The Violet Flame can help considerably. Any effort made by any individual to help with this settlement makes a huge difference to our world.

CHAPTER 11

PAST, PRESENT AND FUTURE

From the beginning...

The Violet Flame of Lemuria and Atlantis

One of the earliest civilisations that remains in the consciousness of mankind is Lemuria, an ancient civilisation in the Pacific
Ocean that predates Atlantis. On its eastern shores stood the
City of Angels, now known as Los Angeles and the Temple of
Purity was in the City of 7 Hills, now San Francisco. The part of
California west of the San Andreas Fault was Lemuria. As land
masses shifted and sea levels rose it became attached to the
larger continent. It is perhaps not too great a leap of the
imagination to visualise a city of Angels, with Temples dedicated
to many from the Angelic Realm including Zadkiel and Holy
Amethyst as the Archangels of the Violet Flame.

In Atlantean times too, the Violet Flame was much revered,
and people would go to the healing temples to realign their
physical state with the Violet Light of Spirit. The dis-ease of the
physical body was transmuted to positive health and wellbeing.
The decline of Atlantis is thought to be partly due to the disconnection from their Spiritual source as the human senses
brought experiences that were valued more highly. Temples
fell into ruin or became used for other purposes. At that time
Master Rakoczy, the overseer of all incarnations on Atlantis,
directed St Germain to transport the Violet Flame to safety.

Much of the karma of all great civilisations that rose and fell still affects Earth, and so us too. There is much we can learn about and from these times; it is the history of mankind, our heritage and the journey of all our souls. We can ask Master Rakoczy to increase our awareness of them, that the lessons will be understood and the karma released through the Violet Flame.

This can all be achieved through meditation, writing, drawing, working with crystals, repetition of mantras and decrees – any of the methods that feel right for you personally. There is so much that our focused thought can achieve with the Violet Flame, if we just put our mind to it!

Now...

By calling on the Violet Flame, we are bringing to ourselves and to our Earth:

Mercy
Forgiveness
Justice
Freedom
Transmutation
Sacred Ceremony
And Magic

Just as it was once called the Violet Flame of Freedom, I feel that the greatest freedom we have is the freedom of choice. We can change ourselves, our lives and our world if we choose to. As The Elohim said...

"So you will decide whether the Violet Flame shall be for you, the point of the springboard of your victory, turning around your life and your outlook. Everything that happens to you in this world can be altered by the Violet Flame. Only you can decide!"

So I feel we can now add *Hope* and *Choice* to that list.

Lighten up!

It can be tough going tackling some of life's issues. Any matters that are life-changing are never going to be trivial! However, working with the Violet Flame brings a lightness to even the most serious problem. Do not think it disrespectful to have fun when working with the Violet Flame. The energy always works for the Highest Good, so how we use it can vary greatly to achieve the same result. There are no limits, restrictions or formal rules; you need only an open and honest heart. The more creative you want to be the better – have fun, enjoy working with the Violet Flame – it certainly is not dull or boring!

A friend of mine, Andrew, who also enjoys working with the Violet Flame, shared this method with me recently:

He imagines sitting on a stool in front of curtains which draw apart to reveal a conveyor belt, (just as in an old game show on television where contestants had to remember items that passed, in order to win them as prizes.) On his conveyor belt are items or pictures representing feelings, personality traits, events, people or situations from which he wishes to transmute any negativity. At his side he imagines a Violet Flame gun and zaps them with Violet Flame firing out of the barrel. He admitted to making the gun noises too!

There is someone who knows how to be creative and have fun with it! The intent is honest, the will for it to work is true, and the Violet Flame does the rest.

At the very beginning of this book, I quoted the Elohim, the great cosmic creators, urging us to:

"...whistle the Violet Flame, sing the Violet Flame, jump and dance to the Violet Flame, do circle dances to all of your music to the Violet Flame, create new music to the Violet Flame decrees. Make games out of it! Do marathons with it! But *whatever you do, beloved ones, you have to get busy with exciting and innovative methods to bring that Violet Flame into every area of your life."*

They really do help us in whichever way we choose to work with the Violet Flame. All Spiritual Beings resonate with the frequency or vibration of joy and happiness, for that is where Love is.

...and so it goes on...

The Violet Flame is expanding so fast, both in the world and in individuals who use it. The more aware we become of its spiritual aspects and those Beings who guard and direct it, the greater its effect on our planet. In my next book I explain how the Violet Flame has existed throughout time and space, tracing it back through previous civilisations on Earth and out into the Universe. By connecting with the spiritual aspects of the Violet Flame, increasing knowledge and understanding, we evolve too – becoming the spiritual beings that we are. Wisdom and insights given by the Ascended Masters, Archangels and all those connected with the Violet Flame will help us on that journey. Together we will learn and understand that we are indeed able to co-create our reality.

For more information on books, talks, workshops, courses, and related items visit:

www.thevioletflame.co.uk
or
www.hilarystanley.co.uk

GLOSSARY

Akashic Records – These are the records of all your thoughts, intentions and actions from all incarnations. They are your own private records, written by your Higher Self in absolute truth and honesty. They can be accessed by you to review any outstanding karma.

Alchemists – Scientists of the Middle Ages who attempted to turn base metal into gold. The Spiritual Alchemists used the Violet Flame to transmute our base instincts into spiritual 'gold'.

Alchemy – This is the science of transmutation; where the rule of physics that 'energy moves matter' is taken further to a state of 'energy alters matter'.

Archangel Zadkiel and Holy Amethyst – They are the Angelic Guardians and Directors of the Violet Flame. They are the Archangels of the Seventh Ray (Violet) who preside over a host of Violet Flame Angels.

Archeia – These are the female counterparts of the Archangels, commonly referred to as their 'twin flames'. For example: Holy Amethyst is Archangel Zadkiel's Archeia.

Ascend/Ascension – This is the aim of those incarnated on this Earth: to achieve enlightenment and rise above their physical state. This can be attained at the end of their physical lives when all lessons have been learnt and karma balanced so that they may reside purely in a spiritual state.

Ascended Masters – Beings who have attained their Ascension after living many lifetimes. They chose to remain close to the Earth plane in order to teach and guide people who are still learning through living physical lives.

Atlantis – Believed to be an advanced civilisation here on Earth that existed in the Atlantic Ocean but was flooded by the rising seas at the end of the Ice Age. The Violet Flame of Freedom was revered in its Temples until it was removed to safety by St. Germain at Master Rakoczy's direction. They considered that this ancient society had become so corrupt that its downfall was inevitable.

Aura – The energy field of any living thing that surrounds the physical form. It is not usually seen with the naked eye.

Chakras – These are energy centres within the body through which the Meridian energy lines flow. They are like stations on a railway line through which a lot of energy passes and so can sometimes become blocked.

Dimensions – We are familiar with the three dimensions of height, width and depth and these are the dimensions that we see and use to understand our world. Beyond these are Space and Time; that is the space or volume that an object occupies and the time that it is there. Beyond this, unrestricted by our understanding, are many other dimensions which include universal concepts and spiritual realms which cannot be measured against our limited dimensions.

Elohim – These are Cosmic Beings that carry the highest concentration of Spiritual Light that we can comprehend. They are the builders of form and structure creating things of a tangible nature out of pure energy, even bringing whole worlds into being. The Elohim inspire us to be creative. Arcturus and Victoria are the Elohim strongly connected to the Violet Flame.

Etheric Realms – These are the layers of Earth's aura or energy field which are not seen or felt in the physical sense. They can be imagined as above the cloud layer but within the blue of our atmosphere.

Freedom Flame – It is a flame or a flaming torch that is the visual representation of freedom. One such flame is held by the Statue of Liberty in New York harbour to indicate that America was a land of freedom or liberty. The Freedom Flame is the colour of violet.

Grounded – The term used to describe feeling stable, secure and connected to the Earth.

Guardians and Directors – Spiritual Beings, such as Ascended Masters and Archangels, who guard or keep safe sacred knowledge and wisdom, and all those who use it. They direct spiritual energy to whoever or wherever it is requested, if it is for the Highest Good.

Guides – Spiritual Beings who help and guide us to achieve our Life's Purpose. They have usually lived many human lives in order to learn and gain the wisdom to guide those who are still going through their evolutionary journey.

Hara Centre – It is considered the physical centre of gravity of the human body and is positioned just below the waistline.

Heart Chakra – This is the energy centre at your heart which is linked to the emotions and is depicted as the colour green with pink at the centre.

Higher Self – This is the part of you that remains in spirit when you incarnate, the higher consciousness of all your physical and spiritual energy throughout Time and Space.

Highest Good – This is the term used to describe when something is for the 'good of all' rather than just personal gratification. It is also referred to when something happens that is beyond present wishes like a 'blessing in disguise'. This also goes beyond Time and sometimes is only seen with hindsight.

Invoke – To call upon or to summon by magical means or prayer.

Justice Flame – A flame or a flaming torch that is the visual representation of justice. The Justice Flame is the colours of purple and gold.

Karma – This is the word frequently used to describe the balance or imbalance of all our actions and intentions throughout our many lifetimes.

Kuan Yin – An Ascended Master and one of the Lords of Karma. She is the Goddess of Mercy and Compassion revered throughout the Far East. She presided over the Seventh, or Violet, Ray for two thousand years.

Lady Portia – The Ascended Master and twin flame of St Germain with whom she is the current overseer of the Violet Flame for this two thousand year period. She carries the scales of justice and the sword of truth. She is also one of the Lords of Karma.

Lemniscate – The infinity symbol, like a figure of eight on its side that is a perpetual loop of moving energy throughout Time.

Lemuria – An ancient civilisation on Earth said to reside in the Pacific Ocean before the time of Atlantis.

Light Beings – The energy of light concentrated enough to become conscious without having physical form. This includes Guides and Beings of other realms such as Angelic or Elemental, who are usually only seen by those with psychic vision.

Lords of Karma – These are Spiritual Guides who have chosen to help us with the issue of Karma alongside their other, individual areas of authority.

Mandala – The name given to any pattern formed to hold the focus of a specific intent such as healing.

Manifestation – Setting the intent to bring into physical reality your desires, in alignment with the Highest Good. It also refers to the sudden appearance of something that had not previously been noticed.

Master Rakoczy – (aka: Master R, or The Great Divine Director) He was the Ascended Master who held the blueprint plans for the entire evolution of souls on Atlantis. He directed St Germain to transport the Violet Flame to safety when Atlantis submerged. He is also one of the Lords of Karma.

Mercy Flame – The visual representation of the intense compassion and understanding held by Kuan Yin. The Mercy Flame is the colour of orchid pink.

Meridian lines – Invisible lines of energy that run throughout the body, known of and used in healing practices for thousands of years, particularly in the Far East.

Merlin – An incarnation of St Germain as King Arthur's alchemist, prophet and advisor. He is recognised in his own right as keeping alive the element of magic in the Violet Flame.

Omri-Tas – The Ruler of the Violet Planet who presides over 144,000 priests and priestesses who tend the Violet Flame in Temples all over the Violet Planet and here on Earth in the Etheric Realms.

Reiki – A method of 'hands-on' healing. It draws on the natural life force energy of all living things to increase the flow of energy along the Meridian lines and particularly through the Chakras.

Ripple effect – This describes energy that radiates out from a thought or action creating an effect on others or the surroundings throughout time; rather like dropping a pebble in a pond.

Scrying – A method of divination focusing on water, an object or flame to stimulate psychic vision.

Spirit – The term used to collectively describe all those who have passed from this physical life, as well as Guides, Guardians and Higher Beings. It is also used to describe our own non-physical or Higher Self.

Spirit and Soul – I believe that the Soul is the pure essence of energy that separates from Source, the 'divine spark'. The Spirit is the energy that is our Higher Self, going through incarnations and travelling through all Realms and Dimensions, holding and protecting the Soul. These two can become damaged and the Violet Flame repairs and restores them.

Soul Group – This is the group of souls with whom we most often choose to reincarnate. Our family members and friends are usually from this group as are people we meet who make a difference to our journey through life.

Solar Plexus – The Chakra centre between the lower ribs in the centre of the midriff. It is depicted as the colour yellow and is a centre of strength and determination.

Source – This is a term sometimes used as an alternative to 'God'. It implies the origin or creation of all energy. It is pure unconditional love. Every thought, action, matter, and all Life are formed out of this energy.

St Germain – The twin flame of Lady Portia and the Ascended Master most commonly called upon for, and most closely associated with, the Violet Flame. He took over the Seventh Ray office from Kuan Yin and is the current Guardian and Director of the Violet Flame.

Transform – To undergo a change in form, appearance, or character. To alter the nature, function, or condition of anything. Transformation can occur spontaneously, with or without conscious action.

Transmute – To cause a change from one state to another. Transmutation is to convert by conscious thought or action, with intent, to cause a transformation to occur.

Twin Flame – This is the phrase used to describe one soul that splits into two, much like the way that cells divide at conception. These are best understood as male and female as that is the closest concept that we can understand them to be.

Vibrational frequency – Everything in the Universe vibrates. The vibrational frequency is the speed, range and complexity of those vibrations.

Violet Flame Temple – There have been many Violet Flame Temples on Lemuria, Atlantis and the Violet Planet. They still exist in the Etheric Realms of Earth and are places where the Violet Flame is kept burning.

Violet Planet – This is a planet that was much like Earth. It was transformed into a world free from disharmony, disunity and distress by the energy of the Violet Flame. It has an aura of Violet Light. It is not in our solar system.

Violet Ray – Pure white light can be separated into frequencies which appear as different colours. The coloured bands of Light are referred to as Rays and each Ray of Light has its own energetic quality. The Violet Ray has the attribute of transformation. In spiritual terms, these colour Rays resonate with the energy of 'Light Beings', such as Ascended Masters, Archangels, and the Elohim. For example, the Archangel of the Violet Ray is Zadkiel because his energy and that of Violet Light are the same frequency.

ACKNOWLEDGEMENTS

With grateful thanks to:

Emma Cutler for her endless support, help, advice and encouragement.

Hilary and Mark at the School of Inner Light for the introduction to the Violet Flame.
www.schoolofinnerlight.co.uk

Ian Thorp for his interest and help in publishing this book – Talking Stick is an imprint of Archive Publishing.
www.transpersonalbooks.com

Jeni Powell for the Violet Flame aura sprays.
www.crystalbalance.co.uk
jeni@crystalbalance.co.uk

Jennifer Sheldon for proof reading and editing.
jennifersheldon@btconnect.com

Kate Gowrie for creating the logo in a digital format from Hilary's original design.
kate.gowrie@gmail.com

Lisa Cutler for taking my photograph for the back cover.
www.lisacutler.co.uk
lisa@lisacutler.co.uk

Samantha Belara Logan-Hochadel for the Violet Flame aura sprays.
www.fulfilledwishes.com
talktome@fulfilledwishes.com

Walter Bruneel for the cover image.
Visionary Artist - Energy Practitioner & Teacher
www.walterbruneel.com
walterbruneel888@gmail.com

And all those who have offered their own experiences and stories to be shared.